EXCUSES, EXCUSES

EXCUSES, EXCUSES

Or How To Get Out of Doing Practically Everything

By Robert A. Myers

BELL PUBLISHING COMPANY
New York

This edition is published by Bell Publishing Company,
distributed by Crown Publishers, Inc.,
by arrangement with The Citadel Press.
h g f e d c b
BELL 1981 EDITION
Manufactured in the United States of America

Library of Congress Cataloging in Publication Data

Myers, Robert, 1932–
    Excuses, excuses, or, How to get out of
doing practically everything.

    1. Excuses—Anecdotes, facetiae, satire, etc.
I. Title.
[PN6231.E87M9   1981]   818'5402   81-10076
ISBN 0-517-35293-1   AACR2

To MONIKA, ANNA and PHILIP

You will always be my best excuse

CONTENTS

EXCUSES, EXCUSES

Introduction

Having to Say You're Sorry

◅§ What matters most is the living of our own lives—playing with our kids, making love, reading books, following our sports and hobbies, and cultivating the vital art of doing nothing. But just saying *no* is rarely the best way to clear the hurdles to our pursuit of these admirable ends. While *I don't want to* (generally reducible to *I'm bored, tired, scared, hostile* or *hungry*) is a sentiment that we rush to accommodate when signaled by our dogs or cats, among bipeds it is only the most slobberingly extravagant devotion that is truly "never having to say you're sorry." If you doubt this, consider how many unblinking *I don't want to's* you can get away with during a week's span. "I just don't *want* to come to work!" "I just don't *want* your sister here at Easter!" "I just don't *want* to take you to that musical!" Indeed, the "white lie" is the essential grease of most interhuman relations. Doubtless partygoing can become a bore, but to put it just that way to an anxious host who has spent hard-earned cash to guarantee a winning evening is to run the risk of being blackballed from all his parties—including that next one that all your buddies will be flocking to. And it should be obvious that in the bedroom a hundred "headaches" beat one flat-out "No!" all hollow.

While this book might have been presented as a mere survey of widely used or very clever excuses (it is that too) or as a cool inquiry into some principles governing their application (it is also that), it was clear from the start that such bland packaging would be seen through as the feeblest of hypocrisies, i.e., as a lousy excuse. Plainly such a work's main appeal would have to lie in its promise of expertise in a critical area where failure may invite nasty consequences, whether that promise was professed or not. So consider it professed.

How to Make This Book Work for You

No book could give all the excuses as the possibilities are as wide as the world and as deep as life itself. Nor does this one even claim to tell you much that you haven't heard already. What it does offer is a useful assortment of memory-joggers. It plays back things you've often thought of saying to somebody, usually when the ripe moment has withered, and the many more things you've heard others say—those airtight, unarguable nuggets that serve the rotten occasion so perfectly and leave one free to move on to more important matters.

However, even the best of excuses is foredoomed unless careful attention is paid to the following points.

Selling the Excuse

Excusemanship is a selling job and requires the same curious mixture of clinical detachment and total commitment that a political candidate brings to his platform, a trial lawyer to his defense, an advertiser to his campaign. The attorney who broods too long on the "truth" of a case is a likely loser. The sharper shyster commands his client, "Never tell me whether or not you really bludgeoned that old man." Such irrelevancies only slow down his attempt to build an argument that will mesh with the shibboleths of jurisprudence and satisfy a jury's unreasonable lust for utter reasonableness. And why should the ad man fret about rumored carcinogens in a casserole when that yummy, cheesy layout is about to cancel out his past three flops? The point is, once you've decided to launch your attack, then why not succeed at it?

Furthermore, excuse-making itself is the very nub of every good sales pitch. Since greed is a basic human trait, the salesman usually has little trouble in making you desire his wares. His real task is to create, in your behalf, a pretext that will enable you to sweep away your own hateful resistances to the gratification of that desire. In the same way, your boss or spouse or friend wants like hell to believe you. Not to believe means anxiety, decision-making, and painful reprisals. People cry out to be convinced.

However, to be a good salesman you must sell not only the excuse but also yourself. You must make yourself liked, and to do this you must manage to like your mark. Dale Carnegie got rich on that principle: putting the focus on the other guy. You must make him feel important, let him talk, adapt to his mood, understand his needs, *like him!*

> *"Hi, Boss. I'm miserable about missing that conference with the new suppliers, but I've got the ripest cold you've ever seen. I've tried NyQuill and a gallon of orange juice, but I can't seem to kick the sneezes and the sopping runnies. I couldn't drag myself in if I tried—and if I did I'd probably queer the deal for you. Thanks for your sympathy. What's that? I ought to take honey and lemon with whisky? Boss, that sounds fantastic, I'll give it a whirl! Well, since I'm probably going to be out the rest of the week, I'll try to use the down time to advantage . . . like reading up on those new contract requirements. And can I call you tomorrow to find out what happened on that deal? I'd hate to be left in the dark."*

THE CONTEXT

You can say anything to strangers and be believed, but when your excusees are the folks you deal with every day—and most are—then it is vital that you conform to their fixed notions of your quirks, capacities, and limitations. What your friend or employer is apt to buy may sound like pure piffle to your brother or spouse. Much also depends upon the age, IQ, and sophistication of your listener, as well as his mood on that particular day. What aided you in bugging out the last time may ensnare you this time.

It is equally important that your reading of the occasion be sensitive and accurate. Arriving a half hour late for a poker game is not the same thing as missing your kid sister's five-thousand-dollar wedding and catered reception.

SPECIFIC DETAILS

A poor excuse is rightly called transparent. Bald clichés like "Something's on the stove," "I'm under the weather," or "I had a flat tire" not only fail to convince, but they prompt their recipient to focus upon you instead, making him wonder what your real reason might be—and how much longer you are going to milk it. Furthermore, his intelligence is insulted and he may try to get you. Yet its amazing how a touch of specific detail can transfuse the moldiest chestnut with the kind of charming real-life quirkiness that wins sympathy. Take that "flat tire." Now, in these days of good roads and belted radials, flats—especially blowouts—are pretty rare. So why not play upon that very unusualness, even build it up?

> *"You know, one of my worst fears is having a blowout on the turnpike at sixty-five. So guess what, it happened to me this morning and I'm here to talk about it. It was my right rear tire, and it just popped open—blammo!—and luckily I managed to stop on the siding without getting clobbered or even wrecking my wheel-rim. I couldn't believe it since that tire had six layers of polyester and fiberglass. Well, what happened was that one had gone completely bald and worn a hole the size of your hand right down to the last remaining threads, and I just hadn't noticed. I guess it pays to check your tread."*

Now you have probably caught your man's ear, and touched a few personal chords as well, since such happenings are almost everybody's daily dread. Also you have entertained him. If he wants more details, and you have taken the time to polish your script, you can go on about your fumbling attempts with a jack and lug-wrench and your long stroll up the siding in search of a call box.

PLANNING AHEAD

The excuses in this book are grouped into two main sections, *The Catch-Alls* and *Special Problems*. While one of the Special Problems listings—say, "Dodging Invitations"—may meet your present needs, it is just as likely that a "Medical" or "Children" Catch-All will work twice as well. Thus you are urged to start by reading this volume through from cover to cover, checking off *all* the best and most fitting items as you go along. Having done this, go back and jot little extra touches into the margins and index them by writing page numbers on the flyleaf. (For maximum efficiency you might also paste tabs onto key pages.) Only now are you really ready to nail this book down beside your telephone.

If time permits, try more sophisticated pre-planning. For instance, a strained ligament will be doubly believable if you tell your boss at quitting time that you are on your way to your weekly karate lesson.

About the Telephone

It is a safe bet that you will phone in most of your excuses, and that should work in your favor. To begin with, the telephone (using the jargon of Marshall McLuhan's media analyses) is a "hot medium" that, within a very narrow sensory spectrum, commands absolute attention and respect. Consider the last time you made an appointment to see someone on urgent business. You woke up early, drove many miles, waited twenty minutes in an outer office, and when you finally got into your conversation, the buzzer on your man's desk sounded and he picked up his receiver and spoke into it slavishly for half your allotted time despite the fact that the caller was plainly some looney who had reached the wrong department. There is something in that buzz or jingle that can trigger the wildest oscillations between our fears and desires. "Could it be my wife about tonight's tickets—my boss about that salary increase?— my bookie about the fourth race at Caliente?" Anything and everything is possible. And even when we are not intimidated but are instead determined to sign off at the first opportunity, an odd unspoken etiquette often makes that most difficult. Certain shutdown signals must be received before we can drive in the closing wedge: "Sure . . . fine . . . so, until then. . . ." We feel it just as keenly when we're on the calling end, this extension of ourselves through the arrogance of technology. There's no way our man can stroll around us as if we were a steer at auction, inspecting our lines and blemishes, and then begin to dissipate our presence with fidgety glances at his snotty quartz watch. No, he's hooked onto our hotline and hasn't the guts to come up with a flat "Not interested— goodbye!"

Practically speaking, we can feed him most anything and be believed, especially since the advent of method acting, which goes against the grain of stereotyped expectations. Who can tell if the most normal delivery isn't tinged with flu viruses when those viruses are said to be swarming there? And when we choose to hedge our bet and fake symptoms, even the hammiest talking-through-the-nose cold can sound wholly convincing through the fuzz and static of today's overloaded phone circuits. Any amateurish stab at the Godfather's rasp can win a case for laryngitis, hiccups are easier, and most everybody can simulate fatigue without half trying. So the telephone is your best bet, and no one can see your golf shoes or the finger you're giving the establishment.

A Caveat Emptor

With all the best intentions, a few perverse souls will go on bungling every excuse. Though they come armed with the good ones, the crucial moment will always find them betraying insincerity, confusion, and loss of nerve. If you honestly know yourself to be one of these uninstructables, then we strongly advise you to cling to your old line of no-saying or not-saying as a smidgen less self-destructive than making a constant ass of yourself.

Observation reveals that such ineptitude is usually rooted in a hatred of excuses derived from being on the receiving end too long. Thus it is most common among employers, parents, creditors, paupers, cops, and uglies. If one of these shoes fits you, then you are equally well advised not to throw this book out but instead to master its contents all the more zealously as a means of combating your deceivers and exploiters.

Acknowledgments

Specific mention of all those people—friends, relatives, colleagues, and total strangers—whose fancies and experiences were the raw material of this survey would run to beyond three thousand names, so a blanket Thank You One and All will have to suffice.

PART ONE

THE
CATCH-ALLS

The lion's share of blame for our not-being-there-as-expected goes to our illnesses, our cars, our families, our jobs, our houses, our pets, and our friends. While excuses from each of these categories are amply served up in the following pages, the reader is cautioned to pick and choose among them in terms of their probable time consumption. He should carry in his head a kind of movie critic's one-to-four-star rating scale ranging from, say, *minor* (good for an hour's to half a day's delay) to *important* (out all day) to *major* ("Call me in three days") to *disastrous* ("Don't send flowers").

CHAPTER *1*

Medical

⬅§ Be cautious when calling in sick. Your boss is likely to be older than you, thus considerably one-up in medical experience. Also, in view of the alarming industrial losses attributed to absenteeism in recent years, he has probably acquired a kneejerk skepticism. Chances are he will ask you about your symptoms, your prognosis, and your prescription ("What *kind* of pills?"). If he is truly the paranoid type, he may even send a spy over to see whether you are really wilting in bed and not out in the back yard building that new retaining wall. At the very least, he may demand that you show him a certificate of illness from your physician. We trust you and your doctor are on the best of terms.

A good general rule is to be prepared for anything. If you have to plead sick, try to make it an illness you have already had, whose characteristics are second nature to you. And if you can establish a multi-use affliction like ulcers, arthritis, or chronic backache, all the better—or all the worse if they are for real. Whatever happens, do take note of all the little credibility-clinching details we have supplied for the excuses you are about to read. Also consult the "Guidelines to Current Remedies" at the end of this chapter.

General Complaints

I've had a hundred-and-one temperature for the past three days, yet nothing specific seems to be wrong with me. My doctor wants me to stop by for a fast check.

My old hay fever hit me and I'm dripping like a faucet. I'm going out now to buy some Allerest.

The Allerest made me too dopey to drive.

I punctured my hand on a rusty nail. It's been years since my my last tetanus booster, so I'd better head in for some professional treatment.

My neck is so stiff I can't turn my head. The doc thinks it's a kind of virus cold in the muscles, and he wants me to try some little green pills that are supposed to ease the tension.

I can't shake the hiccups. It's ridiculous and embarrassing, but really no joke. My larynx feels sore as hell, like it's in shreds. (You are taking those same little green muscle-relaxing pills. And don't forget to hic three times.)

My eyes have been bothering me. They well up when I'm driving and I get headaches when I read. My physician has set up an appointment for me with an oculist. I may need glasses. (Later say you are only taking special eye exercises.)

I was lying by the pool and romancing a martini when all of a sudden I felt a sting on my left earlobe. It turned out to be a bite from a red ant, and right now I'm having trouble keeping my sense of balance.

My hemorrhoids kept me up half the night. I've been using Petrosyllium, that gooey stuff that softens up your stool, and also Preparation H, but nothing seems to dull the ripping pain. I'm hoping I won't need a hemorrhoidectomy. They say it's murder.

That was a super party you hosted, but I've got a monumental hangover. Do you have any good remedies to suggest? (Everybody has.)

I've been constipated all week, which has resulted in nausea, heartburn, heachaches, and a pain in the rectum from trying too hard. My doc wants me to knock off work for a day or two; he says I should take enemas, do some exercises, and chug lots of fluids and milk of magnesia. (Other medications: petrolatum-and-agar and aromatic cascara sagrada.)

I've got the juiciest cold you've ever seen. I'm staying in bed and drinking lots of liquids, the whole shot.

Frankly I'm zonked. At first I thought it was just overwork and lack of sleep, but I can't seem to snap back. I'm about to get checked out for mononucleosis. I mean I'm really beat. (Later it turns out to be a vitamin deficiency.)

Your mountain cabin sounds great, but with my emphysema I stop breathing at 4,000 feet.

The cocktails would only make my canker sores hurt worse.

My trick vertebra went out. My wife is going to drive me over to the chiropractor's.

I'm supposed to drop by the doctor's office with a specimen, but so far nothing has happened.

He wants a semen specimen for his progress check on my vasectomy, but he forgot to lend me any dirty pictures.

As I was lugging a twenty-pound turkey out of the freezer, it slipped out of my hands and fell on my foot. My big toe throbbed so badly I couldn't sleep all night, and this morning it's double-sized and all purple. I'm heading for the clinic to get it set. (Later it isn't broken after all, but you have to walk very cautiously.)

Did you know that I've been wearing orthopedic shoes? Well, last night they got stolen and now I can't walk for five minutes without a shooting pain in my back. I'm on my out to buy some new ones. (Later a pair of special arch supports turn out to be just as effective.)

Did you know that I caught a touch of malaria when I was in Vietnam? Well, the other day I got a recurrence—felt chilled and started shaking like a leaf, then went into a high fever. Right now I'm dripping with sweat and feeling weak as a guppy. I'm on Chloraquine phosphate (or pentaquine, primaquine, quinacrine).

Yesterday I sacked out on the beach for three hours, and today the tops of my feet are so red and swollen I can't even put my shoes on. The doctor is giving me some special cortisone lotion.

Being a lousy swimmer I shouldn't have, but I swam about thirty yards out and got caught in an undertow and had to be hauled in by a lifeguard. Afterwards I went into a state of shock and had to have a blood transfusion. Right now I'm resting in bed.

I drove out into the desert and ran out of gas. After the four-mile hike back to the highway I practically collapsed from loss of body salt through perspiring. I've got to stay home and rest and keep eating salt tablets.

I've got a touch of diarrhea. (Usually this embarrassing statement precludes further questioning. If not, try more colorful variations like "I've got the screaming runners," "I've been on the throne for the past two hours," etc.) You see, I went up in a Piper Cub yesterday and I think the change in atmospheric pressure brought it on. I'm taking Kaopectate. (Other causes of short-term diarrhea: too much rich, weird food or drink, especially on a plane or boat; a new fad diet; emotional stress; a visit to another city and consequent reaction to different virus strains in the drinking water.)

I went over the border for one of those big cheap Mexican dinners, and the next day I had to hit the john about eighteen times. Right, it's bona fide Montezuma's Revenge, with no end in sight. It looks like I'll be out all week on a steady diet of Tetracycline, if I don't die first. And please don't pay me a visit. The smells around here are devastating. (Also identified as Jelly Belly, the G.I. Trots, Tourista, etc.)

Hello, Boss, how are you feeling? Okay? Boy, am I glad to hear that! That bug is really going around and I thought you might have what I've got. I feel like there's a hundred pounds on my back. Headache, stomach ache, sore all over and burning up with a fever of 103. Yeah, I'm popping the old penicillins. Say, if you feel at all woozy you ought to head for home yourself. Well, I'll try to call you back in a couple of days to see how you are and let you know how I'm faring. (Try to specify the strain of your flu— London, Hong Kong, A-Victoria, Australian, Swine, etc., etc.)

You know that flu I thought I'd finally kicked? Well, it seems to have escalated into walking pneumonia.

I started seeing light flashes and then I got this nasty pain in the left side of my head. Also I'm sick to my stomach. I tried aspirin, but that didn't do it one bit. My doctor thinks it's a migraine and he insists on warm baths and a lot of rest. He's giving me Ergotrate.

My regular EKG was okay, but I shouldn't try anything that strenuous until I've taken another one on the treadmill.

A friend of mine who's a health-food freak made me drink some raw goat's milk, and ever since then I've been getting weird pains in my muscles and fever and chills. The doc thinks its brucellosis and wants me to stay home for a few days and take some antibiotics.

This morning I coughed up a drop of blood.

For Women Only

Male friends and bosses will rarely dare to question these. Other women can prove super-inquisitive.

We've been trying *coitus interruptus*, and this morning I threw up and fainted. My husband wants me to take the rabbit test right away.

I tried using an intrauterine device and now I'm bleeding and getting cramps.

I can't seem to menstruate at all. This could be due to a glandular problem or it could mean I'm anemic. I feel like checking it out right away. (The medical term for this is amenorrhea.)

I menstruate too much. I'm told that this can be serious as it might be due to a tumor or polyp. Sometimes the uterus has to be scraped. (Med: menorrhagia)

I get awful pains when I menstruate. My doctor thinks it might be caused by emotional factors. He's giving me sedatives and analgesics. (Med.: dysmenorrhea)

My breasts have been inflamed for a week. (Med.: mastitis)

I've detected a tiny lump in the left one.

I've got the kind of vaginal discharge that is caused by tricho-
monas, meaning my husband and I both have to go in for treatment.

Those involuntary contractions just won't stop. (Med.: vagin-
ismus)

Cosmetic

Sheer ickiness—often more gruesome in the telling than in the
seeing—is the message here, summoning up visions of lost sales,
lowered office morale, and spoiled parties. People will rush to honor
your self-imposed quarantine, and even the most devoted lover will
respect your wish not to be seen other than at your beautiful best.

I have a boil on the tip of my nose. It's ready to pop.

My left ear got inflamed and now it's swollen to double its
normal size. I feel like crawling into a hole.

I've got hives—big gory welts all over my face and body. It
could be something I ate. I'm told the best thing for me to do is lie
in lukewarm bath water spiked with Linit starch. Call me in a
couple of days.

I'm a beaut with red scallops all over my skin, covered by
layers of shiny silver scales. Also my hair is falling out in patches
and there are sores all over my feet. My doctor says it's psoriasis
and he thinks it may be basically an emotional problem. I'm using
some cortisone ointment.

I've got eczema all over my arms and part of my neck. You
know, those big scaly dripping patches. I'm trying calamine lotion
to get rid of the itching, which is really terrible.

I've got a hideous sty in my eye. I'm using hot compresses.

Can't we wait until my ringworm goes away?

The Use of Props

I've almost kicked that cold. (Carry a mini-pack of Kleenex and blow your nose often.)

I had a nasty ear infection. (Return to work with a wad of cotton in your ear.)

I might have lost this eye. (Wear an eyepatch.)

The suppurating has stopped, so I guess my wound is on the mend. (Adorn it with artful and touching bandages.)

At first I thought I fractured my ankle, but it was only a bad sprain. (Return with a big Ace bandage and possibly a cane.)

Many drug stores rent canes and crutches. Abbey Rents and other medical-supply outlets offer even more exotic walk-aids as well as wheelchairs, commode chairs, neck braces, traction kits, motorized hospital beds, respirators, humidifiers, whirlpool baths, intravenous stands, sitzbath outfits, gurneys, and a wide assortment of exercisers.

And don't forget to ask your boss where to go for the insurance forms!

Dental

I lost a giant filling and I'm climbing the walls. My dentist says he'll work on me today, but it will involve a long wait.

I had a wisdom tooth pulled out. It was a rough one and required sodium pentothal, and now I'm so tanked up with the stuff I'm high as a kite.

I've had this horrible shooting pain up my left cheek. My dentist thinks one of my bicuspids is abscessed or already dead. He just gave me a prescription for Empirin 3 and arranged for me to see an endodontist tomorrow. That's right, I'm in for a root canal job. I hear it's a painful process, so don't expect me in till Wednesday.

My regular dentist tried to do the root canal himself, and the idiot goofed and broke his needle off right in my tooth. So here I am, in terrible pain with a jaw the size of a cantaloupe. He's setting up an emergency appointment with an endodontist, but I'm told to expect a two-hour wait.

My toothache started too late in the day for me to get to a dentist, so I bought a fifth of whisky, and now I'm too loaded to drive.

My braces came uncemented and they have to be fixed right away or there goes a thousand bucks down the drain.

My denture split apart. Not only can't I eat, but I look like Walter Brennan. The repair job will take the rest of the day.

Mental

Use these excuses with great discretion. The fame of Freud, Jung, and Dr. Joyce Brothers notwithstanding, too many people still tend to equate non-physical disabilities with malingering, weirdness, and moral turpitude. Consider the fate of Senator Thomas Eagleton.

Ever since I went to that body-awareness workshop, I've become so sexually agressive it frightens me. Let's not meet until I get this thing under control.

My depressive cycle is in full swing. When I'm this way I can't be around people without getting on their nerves and their getting on mine. Be a doll and leave me alone for a day or two.

Something negative came between us the other night, and believe me it had nothing to do with you. Frankly, I ran into my ex-wife and got riled up all over again. Give me an hour to beat my punching bag and I'll be okay.

How could I forget Tuesday's appointment? It's weird but I was so upset all day Monday that Tuesday felt like Monday all day long.

I was just rapping along and suddenly I fell on the floor and began screaming and sobbing. Marvin, my Primal therapist, was very excited and insisted I stay on for another hour. He thinks it's a real breakthrough.

Lately all my dreams seem to be about other people's troubles. Dr. Sperling says that's a strong sign of hostility. He thinks I ought to steer clear of everybody until I've had time to sort out my attitudes.

Due to money troubles I had to quit my analysis right when I was on the brink of finding out why all the men I fall in love with turn out to be bisexual.

I was about to leave for your place when I discovered that I've run out of Reserpine, and I can't reach my doctor for a new prescription.

I can't remember your inviting me. But then I seem to forget everything five minutes after I've heard it. My doctor says I have a mild form of Korsakoff's disease, otherwise known as the amnesic syndrome. That means that the gismos that pump information into my memory-storage system are out of order, maybe due to a nutritional deficiency. I'm taking treatments now and the prospects look good.

That old backache has started up, so I've got to hop over to the biofeedback machine and try to beef up my alpha brainwave production.

My electroencephalogram shows 13-per-second spikes, lots of sharp activitiy in the motor leads, temporal single polyphasic sharp waves, and a long row of sharp waves in the right temporal area. In other words, I'd better stay right here at the clinic.

I've got to go back to the TM center because I can't remember my mantra.

I don't dare leave the house. A little green man out there has a long-range rifle aimed at my front door.

Other People's Ailments

Bad news about our friends and relatives usually comes in the form of terse, emotionally charged phone messages: "Al has a bad pain in the chest. I—I just called the paramedics." Thus we can be more rash in our choice of an illness and far less specific as to its symptoms and prognosis. However, in the case of a very close relative there is a risk that our excusee will get it into his head to send flowers or even visit the hospital, and Dad may not appreciate all those get-well cards, not to mention being sucked into a conspiracy. So there is much to be said for citing more distant kin, preferably someone who lives in another town. The only problem here is that the urgency of your visiting your second cousin Hattie during her bout with the gout may not be immediately apparent to others. Accordingly, a general principle comes into play: THE MORE DIS-TANT THE RELATIVE, THE GRAVER THE ILLNESS. Just as Dad's condition must not invite too much interest, so cousin Hattie's must be practically terminal to warrant your missing a whole day.

(Children's problems are covered in Chapter 2.)

My father-in-law is having a prostectomy. We're going to be busy taking my mother-in-law back and forth between their house and the hospital.

My cousin is epileptic and his wife is afraid he'll have a seizure and hurt himself when she's not around. This is her bingo night and I've been drafted to keep him company.

My aunt has been stuck in a wheelchair ever since her stroke, and this is my day to do her shopping, vacuum her carpets, and read to her from the Bible.

My arthritic uncle has a phobia about doctors. He won't go in for his weekly gold injection unless I force him at gunpoint.

We can't come because the old man is wearing a pacemaker and there are too many microwave ovens in your apartment house.

I suppose I could come and bring Mary with me, but she's only been on the wagon for six months and the sight of your fine martinis might prove too much for her.

The girl next door is all alone and going into labor pains. She can't reach her doctor, her husband's out of town, and neither of us has a drivable car. I may have to be a midwife in about five minutes. Catch you later.

My wife's grandmother finally passed away after a long siege of cancer. I have to drive a hundred miles for the funeral. It'll be an all-day ordeal.

George had a cardiac arrest while he was jogging home from the health-food store.

Guidelines to Current Remedies

ANALGESICS—the pain killers
Although most analgesics take the form of little white tablets, they vary greatly in potency, as follows:

1. *Mild:* Store-bought aspirin, *Excedrin, Anacin, Bufferin,* etc.

2. *Strong: Empirin* and *codeine.* These are prescription items and come in graduated strengths. They are good for sprained ankles, postdental surgery, arthritis, etc. Note that *codeine* can make you constipated and shouldn't be used more than once every six hours and not for more than a day before medical care is underway.

3. *Strongest: Demerol.* Prescribed for hospitalized patients or others in severe pain, this compound should be used sparingly and under medical supervision.

ANTIBIOTICS—the enemies of infectious disease
1. *Tetracycline* (an orange and yellow capsule). This is a good all-around antibiotic for intestinal, upper-respiratory, sinus, ear, skin, and bladder infections.

2. Two other good broad-spectrum drugs are *Penicillin* (a white oval tablet or an injection) and *Erythromycin* (a rosy-pink tablet). There are also some other -*mycins.*

3. A touch more potent than the above is *Ampicillin* (gray and red capsule).

Note: Antibiotic dosages are usually "four tablets right away, four more in twelve hours, and one tablet four times a day for the next four days."

ANTIDIARRHEAL AGENTS—for when you have to keep running to the john for several hours.

1. The favorite drug-store remedies are *Kaopectate* (a chalky white liquid) and *Pepto-Bismol* (pink liquid or tablets). Also *Maalox* and *Lomotil*.

2. *Paregoric* (a whisky-colored syrup). This is effective, and can also be used to prevent diarrhea. As it is an opiate, it adds the blessing of a mild high.

Caution: Serious diarrhea from amebic dysentery calls for serious antibiotics.

ANTIHISTAMINES—for colds, allergies, itching from insect bites, and rashes from contact with certain plants.

1. The cold-killers on your supermarket shelf are many and include *Contac, Dristan, NyQuill*, etc.

2. Your doctor is likely to prescribe *Chlortrimeton*, one tablet three times a day. For especially harsh reactions, he might suggest *Benadryl*, one 50 mg. tablet two to three times a day.

Note: Antihistamines may cause blurred vision and make it unsafe to drive.

CHAPTER **2**

Children

◄§ It might seem that only seasoned and loving parents can fully grasp the urgency of children's afflictions. However, we all started out as kids, and often the most hardened pedophobe will prove so sentimentally vulnerable as to collapse in tears at the mere mention of the croup. And everybody knows what unpredictable little menaces our tots can be.

Medical

We'd sure love to see you, but Molly has the measles and the doctor has advised us not to receive any guests.

Eric has a high fever and he's been vomiting so much that he is completely dehydrated. We'll have to stick by him and keep feeding him 7-up.

Eddie's had asthma attacks before, but this is the first time he's turned blue. We're leaving for the fire station to get him some oxygen.

Mary went into convulsions and then fainted. We've got to get her to the clinic for an electroencephalogram to find out if it's epilepsy.

The baby's scrotum has been swollen for two days. It could be a hernia.

His stool is bloody and tarry. My baby book says that can be a sign of internal hemorrhaging.

Lenore has a high fever and a mouthful of canker sores. She sits and cries with her mouth open, and the saliva just drips out because it hurts her so much to swallow. The doctor thinks it's stomatitis, a virus infection.

The kids both woke up with white spots all over their bodies. It had to happen just when my wife is spending the weekend at her sister's.

We've always regarded Jimmy as just a natural-born loud-mouthed, disruptive, underachieving pain in the neck, but the pediatrician thinks he's a hypermotor child and wants us to hurry over to his office for some tranquilizers and antihistamines.

Little Susie was trying to make a pet out of a big gray rat she found in the cellar. Her appointment at the clinic is an hour from now.

Betty got hit in the head by a softball. The nurse called me to bring her home. She suggests we go directly to emergency for a head X-ray.

I've got to go to the store. The only thing that seems to help Phedra's cough is a syrup of thyme and honey, and we're all out of thyme.

Peter mistook Ex-lax for chocolate kisses.

I must have done a bad job of telling Amy the facts of life because she's been throwing up for three hours.

Philip took a Mars bar to bed and five hundred ants joined him.

Dear Teacher:
Ricky hasn't been to class these past ten days be-cause of an ecological survey study he attended with his Boy Scout troop. While on this field trip he climbed a hill that was covered with poison oak, and two days later his skin erupted. I took him to a derma-

tologist, who gave him medication that made him swell so much he looked like an inflated beach ball. To fight off this edema the doctor tried yet another medication, and this one caused a severe allergenic eruption on top of the poison oak mess, which made Ricky very ill. The doctor says he is ready for school now, if you don't mind his sitting in class with a swollen body covered with scabs.

—Ricky's Mother

An All-Purpose Checklist of Illnesses Common to Children

Adenoids	Cradle Cap	Mumps
Allergies	Croup	Pneumonia
Ammoniacal diaper	Dehydration	Posture problems
Anemia	Diarrhea	Rheumatic fever
Asthma	Ear infection	Ringworm
Athlete's foot	Eczema	Rubella (German
Bladder infection	Growths and cysts	measles)
Bronchitis	Hernia	Sties
Canker sores	Hyperthyroid	Stomatitis
Chicken pox	Hypothyroid	Strep throat
Colds	Impetigo	Tics
Colic	Influenza	Tonsillitis
Colitis	Jaundice	Trench mouth
Constipation	Lice	Whooping cough
Convulsions	Measles	Worms

At Home

The baby wet and I had to change her, wash her off, and calm her down.

Little Billy locked himself in the bathroom and I can't remember how to open the door.

He got his shoes soaking wet and he doesn't have another pair.

Richard ate my paycheck.

He was playing filling station and I have eight gallons of water in my gas tank.

I dropped my glasses in the path of his Motocross bike.

He found my latest *Hustler*, so it's time for us to have that long-awaited discussion on the facts of life.

We're in the Father and Son program, and tonight our living room is the teepee.

Susie took my keys and lost them in the back yard. We haven't mowed the lawn in three weeks, and it's so high I had to crawl around on my hands and knees to keep flattening down the grass. After I found the keys I had to change my good slacks because they were all grass-stained around the knees. Then I had to rinse them out quickly before the stains got settled in.

I caught her playing with the thirty-eight revolver I keep loaded in the nightstand. Right now we're in the middle of a very serious talk.

She is two hours late getting home from school. I've got to go look for her.

Our babysitter had an accident on the way over here, and it's too late to call anybody else.

One of our sitters is sick and the other one just ran off to live in a commune at Taos. I suggested the girl across the street, but my wife says she smokes pot and has about five boyfriends who keep hanging around. We're afraid they would use our house for an orgy or steal our silverware.

My neighbor and I have a kind of babysitting exchange, and tonight I'm getting all five of hers. Would you care to come over and help me keep an eye on the one with the loose stool?

While I was in the bathroom, the toddler I was babysitting unlocked the front door and went out across the busy boulevard. He didn't get hit, but his parents are trying to sue me anyway.

Gerald has started to play with matches, so I can't leave until the sitter arrives.

I'm two weeks overdue on my promise to set up the backyard gym outfit he got for his birthday. It's going to be a hellish all-day job. Have you ever looked at those crazy assembly instructions they give you?

Sorry we were delayed. All week long we've promised them they could watch "The Wizard of Oz" on TV, and we couldn't let them down.

They're watching "Starksy and Hutch" tonight, and I have to stand by and blip out the violent stuff.

Sorry we missed the dinner. Sally made a paper glider out of your invitation.

Ever since they put her in the mentally gifted program, she refuses to associate with your kids.

It's her first date and she wants me to chaperone her at 31 Flavors.

Our discipline problem with Lonnie has reached epidemic proportions. We've tried every psychological gimmick there is, but nothing seems to work, so tonight's the night I use the belt.

He got in a fight and broke the other boy's nose. The kid's father just called to say he is coming over to break *my* nose. I'm searching everywhere for that roll of pennies I put away.

You'll have to excuse his behavior. He is at the "terrible two" stage. (Or "terrible four" or "terrible six" stage, etc.)

At School

This is the evening of Anna's school play. She'll be broken-hearted if we're not there.

I've volunteered to work in the school library. It's a miserably poor district; they need every bit of help they can get.

If I miss today's P.T.A. meeting it will be the third time in a row and Harvey's image will be severely tarnished.

He has collected ten bales of newspapers for the class recycling project, and it's up to me to transport them.

He forgot his lunch, and I have to get it over to the school no later than 11:45.

He is being bussed to a ghetto five miles away, and the bus keeps breaking down.

If I don't drive him over and walk him all the way to the classroom door, he'll be mugged again for his lunch money.

We put him in a Methodist private school and it's ten miles away and there's no bus.

He says his teacher has been abusing him. This afternoon I'm meeting with his teacher and the school principal. It's taken me a week to set up this messy confrontation, so I can't miss it.

His teacher wants me to come by for an emergency conference. She claims that his constant use of obscene four-letter words is corrupting the entire class.

They just called to tell me that he swallowed a ping pong ball. Got to run.

At Large

Little Tim got separated from us in that big new shopping mall. We searched all over for him but had no luck because it turned out that he had gone out to the parking lot and, not finding our car, had tried to walk home alone. We called the cops and one of their men spotted him two hours later. We're emotionally exhausted.

While we were idling in the parking lot, Sonny threw the gear into reverse and we smashed into the grille of a new Mercedes-Benz. Should I claim we were rear-ended and try to collect?

He's been stealing candy at the supermarket. Their Man in Blue is threatening to call the cops, so I'd better get over there and try to square things.

Without my realizing it, Adam dropped half a dozen matchbox cars into my overcoat pocket. Right now the store dectective is booking me for shoplifting.

I have to drive my daughter and five of her friends to their church camp, which is forty miles away. Tomorrow I have to drive out there again and bring them back.

They want to see "Silent Movie," so I have to go along and read them the captions.

We're thinking of adopting a Vietnamese war orphan, so we have to go over to the government building and sign some papers.

I'd be a great mother if the kids didn't take up so much of my time.

Excuses to Kids

It's for your own good.

You're not quite old enough.

I'll have to talk that over with your father before giving my consent.

Your mother is against it.

Sure you can go, after you've done your household chores. And I mean *all* of them.

I'll reconsider it after I've seen a drastic change in your behavior.

When you treat other people in that crummy way, you can expect to get the same kind of treatment yourself.

You can't do that without parental supervision, and I'm going to be gone for the afternoon.

I think you're coming down with a cold, so you'll have to stay indoors.

Merry-go-rounds are for little guys, not for big fellows like you.

You know your father and I can't stand Disney movies.

Sorry, but that movie is rated "R."

The place we're going to has a bar, which means no kids allowed.

My dad never got me a bike till I was thirteen, and I had to pay for half of it out of my quarter-a-week allowance.

You can't have it now because that's what Santa's going to bring you for Christmas.

Filet mignon is too rich for kids. Why not try the ground beef patty instead?

Billy Peckwith drinks all his milk, so why can't you?

Grandma would be very disappointed if you didn't make an effort to like her rhubarb pie.

That zucchini is terrific stuff—loaded with vitamins.

The doctor says all that candy is bad for your asthsma.

Tell the non-reading child that the "Yes We Are Open" sign says "No Ice Cream Today."

Kids' Favorites

There are lumps in the Cream of Wheat.

There are clams in the chowder.

I can't sleep without my Donald Duck nightlight.

I can't sleep when you're watching television.

Every time I fall asleep, little brother comes in and wakes me up.

Sister forced me to do it.

She hit me first.

No, he hit me first.

I broke his Six Million Dollar Man because he broke Barbie.

Why do I have to do it when she doesn't?

I feel too sick to go to school.

The teacher gave us homework, but she didn't explain how to do it.

The teacher says we have to watch *Wild Kingdom*.

You didn't give me enough lunch money for a sandwich, so I had to buy a Hostess Twinkie instead.

I can't walk to school because the class bully is waiting to beat me up.

You promised we could watch *Wonder Woman* till nine.

Jeri's mother always lets her watch *Quincy*.

Every time I want to watch *Shazam*, sister gets to watch *Porky Pig*.

You always treat her better than you treat me.

All the other kids get to go.

Haircuts are for sissies.

Everybody laughs at me when I wear that sticky yellow raincoat.

It's too hot to wear my sweater.

I think I made my bed. I can't remember for sure.

I never got to go to a picnic in my whole life.

Dad said I shouldn't.

Mom said I couldn't.

Mom, you keep contradicting yourself.

Nobody told me that the "F" word was bad.

CHAPTER *3*

The Automobile

◄§ If everybody was automotively as much in the dark as you and I, our General Complaints would be sufficient. However, with the current boom in thirfty self-installable auto parts, the amateur greasemonkey is popping up in the most unexpected places, ever ready with advice and a cross-examination. If one of these types crosses your path, and you feel compelled to use one of our Highly Technical excuses, we urge you to be a bit vague at the start: "Gee, the mechanic thinks it might be. . . . "Well, it looks like it could be. . . ." Since you've had car troubles in the past, you know how mystified even the wizards at your corner Exxon station can be about their own diagnoses. (The greatest mystery, of course, is always the bill you receive after the treatment.)

General Complaints

I had a blowout on the freeway. (See page 16 of Introduction.)

I was driving down the freeway when all of a sudden my accelerator stopped working—no power at all. Luckily I was near an off-ramp and managed to coast down to a boulevard. A couple of guys helped me push it across to a Shell station, which is where I am now. It turned out that the spring under the pedal was broken. The mechanic called out to order a replacement, and we're still waiting for it to arrive.

I can't risk driving on the freeway without turn signals. I'll stop at a garage and try to get them fixed fast.

My wife left the headlights on overnight and the battery is dead. I just called Triple A for a quick charge. If it won't hold the charge, I'll try to get a loaner.

My water hose blew. It took me over an hour to attach the spare one I keep in the trunk. (Arrive with a little grease on your hands.)

My fan belt broke.

It was raining and my windshield wipers wouldn't work. It turned out that the wiper control switch was disconnected.

My horn was blaring and I didn't know what wires to pull out.

I started the car, drove fifty feet, and smoke came gushing out of the front end. At that point all systems were not go—the power steering was jammed, the power brakes were kaput, the whole shot. A neighbor of mine thinks it's the coil in the condenser. I'll have it towed to the dealership since I'm still under warranty.

My hot-light flashed red and you'd better believe I stomped on the brakes. The guy in the gas station says my water pump has gone out. Since I can't get a loaner, I'm waiting for someone to pick me up and maybe get me to a bus station, but that'll probably take another hour.

It turned out that the overheating was due to a worn-out thermostat, not the water pump.

The man at Texaco found a carbon monoxide leak in my station wagon. He is replacing all the bolts on the floor.

When I left my car to be serviced, he promised it would be ready by two. Then he went home early and the other guy didn't get started on it till three-thirty. It's still up on the rack with all the wheels off. Looks like I'm in for another hour's wait.

A man in a pickup truck started making a left turn and a kid in a Toyota plowed into his right side. All kinds of people came running up, taking sides about who was in the wrong. Before you knew it, two Highway Patrol units were on the scene, and since I was driving right behind the pickup, I had no choice but to stick around and be a witness.

I was cruising down the freeway and somebody on an overpass dropped a big rock on my car. It tore through the windshield like a cannonball. Although the rock missed my head literally by a hair (if it hadn't I wouldn't be here to tell you about it), I caught a shower of fine glass splinters—all the worse as I was wearing shorts. It took me an hour to get to the hospital and have my legs and private parts vacuumed out, and then I had to report the incident to the police. Naturally the culprit was never found.

My car read hot again, so I pulled over and discovered that my radiator pressure-cap was missing. Somebody must have stolen it during the night.

Some thieves have stripped out my battery and carburetor.

My tires have been deflated.

My car has been stolen. Right now I'm waiting for the cops to arrive so I can make my report. Then I'm off to see my insurance agent. (Make sure you arrive later in a rental car.)

I ran out of gas in a high-crime neighborhood. I was too scared to walk to a gas station in the dark, so I waited for a policeman to notice me. That took a helluva long time. I guess the cops out there are too busy chasing muggers and burglars.

How dumb of me! I locked my keys in my car. It took a mechanic with special "repo" tools a half hour to get the door open.

When I got back to the parking lot, some idiot had parked his Buick in front of my VW and taken his keys. It took the attendant an hour to worm me out of there.

The motor on our automatic garage door broke down. I can't get my car out until the Sears service man arrives.

My father had an emergency and had to borrow my car. He should be back within the hour.

My brother took my car to his auto-shop class to overhaul the brakes.

I tried to repair my own alternator, and now I can't figure out how to get it back together. Nuts and bolts are scattered all over the garage. I may have to call out for assistance.

Some newspapers were bunched up on the garage floor and when I drove in, my catalytic converter set them on fire. It was lucky my gas tank wasn't leaking.

My wife and I had a fight about my going out to the track, and she took the rotor off my distributor.

I just got a notice that my auto insurance has been cancelled. It's all a mistake since I paid them on the first, but I'll have to straighten this out before I dare drive. I'll try to borrow my mother's Subaru.

After that ghastly accident on the highway, I just had to stop off for a stiff straight shot.

I took the 1971 Pinto onto the freeway. My hospital room is 304 in the east wing.

I drive a classic Model-T and I've misplaced the starter crank.

I drive a used British sports car.

My tank is nearly empty and all the local stations are closed on account of the gasoline shortage.

I think the Shell station three miles up the road is open, but if it isn't I won't have enough gas to make it back home.

My wagon is such a gas-guzzler that I won't chance any weekend trip beyond a hundred miles. Unless you can guarantee me a refill!

That station was down to Regular and my new Toyota requires Unleaded.

Highly Technical

MY ENGINE WON'T START

The mechanic thinks it's due to the *open primary ignition circuit*. Specifically: (1) The ignition points are burned or oxidized. (2) The breaker arm is binding on the pivot post, which prevents the closing of the points. (3) The breaker arm is distorted or bent. (4) The ignition switch circuit is open.

He thinks it's due to a *grounded primary ignition circuit*: (1) The insulator at the distributor terminal is cracked. (2) The condensor is grounded. (3) The distributor-to-coil lead is grounded. (4) The primary coil winding is grounded.

He thinks it's a *faulty secondary ignition circuit*: (1) The spark-plug cable terminals are corroded. (2) The ignition coil isn't working. (3) They put in the wrong kind of spark plugs. (4) The distributor cap is cracked.

He thinks there's an *insufficient fuel supply*: (1) The float level is too low. (2) The fuel line to the tank is clogged. (3) The fuel pump camshaft lobe is worn.

He thinks it's the *starter motor*: (1) The starter gear is binding in the flywheel gear. (2) The starter switch is defective. (3) Sludge has built up in the oil.

He thinks it is the *battery*: (1) It's run down. (2) The terminals are loose. (3) The ground is improper. (4) The cables are frayed.

MY CAR IS STALLED

The reason: (1) There are large air leaks in the intake manifold, probably because of a disconnected windshield-wiper vacuum line. (2) It's vapor-locked. (3) The valves were set too tight. (4) There's water in the fuel. (5) The fuel line is frozen.

THE ENGINE STARTS BUT
THE CAR WON'T DRIVE

The reason: (1) There's a broken part in the drive line (anywhere from the clutch to the rear axle shaft). (2) There's not enough oil in the fluid coupling (or torque converter). (3) Something in the automatic transmission is making the clutches bind or drag (or the bands slip). (4) The mixture is too lean (or too rich). (5) The throttle won't open. (6) The exhaust system is clogged.

I'M GETTING NO CHARGE
(Reminder: Cars with generators can be started with a push if the battery is dead; cars with alternators cannot because alternators keep no residual magnetism.)

My *alternator* isn't charging: (1) The drive belt is loose. (2) The brushes are sticking. (3) The charging circuit is open. (4) The connections at the output terminal stud are faulty. (5) The rectifiers are open-circuited.

My *generator* isn't charging: (1) The fan belt is broken (or slips badly). (2) The voltage regulator went out. (3) The brushes are stuck. (4) The commutator is burned (or corroded).

MY ENGINE IS OVERHEATING
The reason: (1) A slipping fan belt. (2) A clogged exhaust system. (3) Late ignition timing. (4) The carburetor mixture is too lean. (5) The water circulation is impeded. (6) The thermostat is busted. (7) One of the water hoses rotted away. (8) The radiator is clogged with road debris. (9) The water pump went out.

MY AUTOMATIC TRANSMISSION ISN'T WORKING
Specifically: (1) The car won't move. (2) It won't upshift in "Drive." (3) It locks up when it upshifts in "Drive." (4) It grunts and groans on take-off. (5) It stalls.

MY MANUAL TRANSMISSION IS IN BAD SHAPE
Specifically: (1) The clutch grabs wildly. (2) The clutch rattles due to a loose flywheel. (3) The clutch is gone.

MY DRUM BRAKES AREN'T WORKING
The reason: (1) Dirty brake fluid. (2) Insufficient or leaking fluid. (3) A bad master cylinder. (4) Grease in the linings. (5) Scored drums or worn linings or a faulty wheel cylinder (resulting in a lot of noise and grabbing).

MY DISC BRAKES AREN'T WORKING

The reason: (1) Insufficient fluid. (2) An air leak. (3) A caliper brake-fluid leak. (4) A damaged caliper piston seal. (5) Improper seating of the piston and shoe and lining assembly.

MY POWER BRAKES ARE OFF

The release is slow or out of order because: (1) The piston return spring is broken. (2) The valve plunger is sticking. (3) The air passage is restricted. (4) There's a piston stroke interference.

I CAN'T STEER THE CAR PROPERLY

It steers erratically when I apply the brakes: (1) A front spring is weak. (2) A steering knuckle is bent. (3) The brakes are out of adjustment.

There's too much play and looseness: (1) The steering gear connections are worn. (2) The steering knuckle bushings are worn. (3) The front wheel bearings (or ball joints or control arm bushings) are worn.

The car keeps pulling to one side: (1) A caster or camber is uneven. (2) The wheel bearings were adjusted too tightly. (3) The frame is bent or broken. (4) The shock absorbers aren't working.

MY OIL PRESSURE IS DANGEROUSLY LOW

The reason: (1) A weak relief-valve spring. (2) Worn oil pump gears. (3) A damaged oil pump gasket. (4) Loose connections in the oil lines. (5) Worn main bearings.

I'M NOT GETTING ANY OIL PRESSURE

The reason: (1) The pressure gauge is broken. (2) The oil pump is defective. (3) The oil pressure relief valve is stuck open.

(For additional car-related mishaps, consult Chapters 8 and 17 and 26.)

Other Modes of Travel

My Kawasaki's front tire got stuck in the streetcar tracks.

The heavy going-home traffic slowed down to forty-five, probably because I look like a motorcycle cop in my new white helmet.

I was afraid to try the freeway in all that pouring rain. I took surface streets instead.

The bus took two hours to get me from there to here. I felt like John Wayne in a covered wagon. I intend to write a nasty letter to the transit authority.

I took the wrong bus and ended up in the next town.

The express bus broke down and they transferred us to the local one.

I fell asleep on the bus and didn't wake up until it reached the end of the line.

Without my reading glasses I can't make heads or tails of those bus schedules.

The cable stopped moving. We had to walk back down from Nob Hill and wait for a bus.

The subway stickup tied us up for five extra stops.

I rented a boat and the outboard motor ran out of gas in the middle of the lake. It took me forever to row back across.

Some friends took us out in their new sailboat, and the damn thing capsized. We had to wait for the Coast Guard.

The navigation charts got swept overboard.

The ferry got into thirty-knot winds and eight-foot swells and, for safety's sake, had to veer five miles off course, which is why I'm later than expected. I feel okay considering that I've been barfing for two hours.

I finally hooked a marlin and the captain gave me an extra hour to try to pull it in.

One of my father's business contacts who works for TWA just gave him a free round-trip ticket to New York. Dad can't go so he's letting me use it this weekend. I'd be a fool not to, since I've never seen the Big Apple and may never get another chance. I'll bring you a souvenir. (Or, if possible, have a postcard relayed back from some friend in Manhattan.)

Our takeoff was delayed on account of a rumor about a sky-jacker.

The only way I could have made it was by air, and I'm deathly afraid of flying.

My cousin took me to Bakersfield in his two-engined Cessna, and when we came back in the evening there was so much fog we couldn't risk a descent. I mean it looked like snow down there. Well, we flew east toward the desert, and it took a half an hour before we finally found a hole. We came down and followed the freeway to Beaumont. We had to land there because the plane was low on gas.

When we landed at that jerky little airstrip, a freakish thing happened: one of the tires went flat. We had no spare, so we had to get the plane towed twenty miles to the nearest town.

A whole truckload of Sears washing machines had spilled onto the tracks just ahead of us. Luckily the engineer saw them just in the nick of time.

Some vandal broke the lock on a switch. It took a yard crew three hours to get us out of that bean field.

They locked the door of the cattle car. From now on I'll stick to hopping gondolas.

My ten-speed derailleur keeps shifting down to first gear and binding there.

I didn't realize it would be an uphill climb all the way.

A car swerved so close that I had to steer into the curb, and I catapulted right over the handlebars. Luckily I'm only bruised.

The building had a power failure and I was stuck in the elevator for an hour.

I had to walk down twenty-three flights of stairs.

The people-mover stopped moving.

The ski-lift stopped lifting.

Our pack horses refused to budge.

The ferris wheel's motor shorted out, and we were stuck up there in the afternoon breeze.

CHAPTER *4*

The House

◦§ While we've been looking the other way, that maze of pipes and wires we call home has grown into a monster capable of swallowing up all our time and equanimity and sometimes knocking us flat.

Crises and Disasters

The hot water heater is gushing a quart a minute. I have to stand guard and keep emptying the bucket.

I just replaced the flex hose, but the new one is the wrong size, so I'll have to make another quick trip to the hardware store.

The dishwasher overflowed and flooded the kitchen floor.

The toilet keeps backing up, and the house smells like a cesspool.

My little brother just found out that you can't flush a cantaloupe down the toilet no mater how hard you stomp on it.

The water pipes inside our bathroom wall disintegrated, and our new bedroom carpet is now a sopping marshland. Luckily our insurance covers indoor water damage.

My husband got his toe stuck in the bathtub faucet. I've tried butter and vaseline, but no luck so far. The plumber is on his way.

I slipped on some soap getting into the bathtub and knocked myself cold. It's lucky I didn't drown.

I left my car keys in one of the pockets of my Levi's, and I can't get at them because the pants are in the dryer and the hatch on the dryer is stuck shut.

My diamond engagement ring slipped off and fell into the garbage disposal. I may have to get the whole unit disassembled.

I put some bread in the toaster and the ejector must have jammed because the toast toasted until it caught on fire and the flames ignited the adjoining wall.

I was three miles up the freeway when I began to wonder whether or not I'd turned off the electric range. It's a good thing I came back because it was on. In another two hours the house might've been reduced to cinders.

Five miles out, my wife thought she had left the bath water running. We came back and she was right.

I decided to rewarm yesterday's beef hash, and how was I to know that the plastic bowl I put it in wasn't heatproof? Right now the kitchen is reeking with toxic fumes and the whole bottom of the oven is covered with sticky yellow gobs. I tried wiping the stuff off, but it's stuck in so tight I'll need a chisel. I'd better get to work on it before my wife comes home.

My freezer broke down. I've just packed fifty filet mignons into a suitcase and I'm on my way out to find a new home for them.

Our new television set just blacked out, and since this is the last day of the ninety-day warranty period, I'll have to dash off to the repair shop.

Our color TV burst into flames. I think I've got the fire out, but now I've got to wait for the firemen to arrive—as usual, too late to do much good.

We made a fire last night, not knowing that some sparrows had built their nest right smack in the top of the chimney. The smoke damage is unbelievable.

My wife was dusting the inside of my gun cabinet and she knocked my twelve-gauge shotgun onto the floor and it blasted a six-inch-wide hole through that Picasso lithograph I've been paying for in installments, not to mention the wallboard behind it.

I went up into the attic to look at the insulation and fell down through the ceiling. I'm not hurt much, but it'll take me several hours to clean up all the debris.

I was trying to mount a new Sparkletts bottle and it slipped out of my hands and burst open on the floor. I mean it exploded—those pieces of glass flew across the room like bomb fragments! Fortunately the kids were in the back yard or they might've been gashed on the leg like I was. Right now the kitchen floor is a lake.

The master bolt on the power mower came loose and that big blade went boomeranging across the yard and chewed up a big hunk of the cedar fence. I've heard of people being decapitated that way.

I came back from the shopping center and found to my horror that the house had been burglarized. They took the tape deck, the stereo receiver, the toaster, the blender, and my husband's Irish porcelain humidor, but they left the console TV, probably because it was too bulky—though they did smash in the picture tube. Would you mind getting off the line so I can call the police and then check out the rest of the house?

Our house got invaded by cockroaches and we called Terminix. The bug men are on their way over now, and we're busy taking everything out of our closets and cupboards so they can spray in there.

Another problem: we just discovered termites in the foundations!

The trash truck has bypassed our house for two weeks and those six full cans are starting to stink up the neighborhood, especially in this heat. I've just rented a pickup truck and I'm about to leave for the city dump.

My shaver broke down, and I'm damned if I'll meet that client looking like Harry the Hobo. Luckily my shaver shop provides loaners, though it's ten miles out of my way.

After I finished painting the living room, I realized that I had used gasoline instead of paint thinner. I'm calling the fire department in advance.

Why the Place Is Such a Mess

I didn't know anybody would be dropping in.

The cleaning lady quit.

The chimney backed up.

We opened some windows to air the place out and a big gust of wind blew in.

The dishwasher broke down and I've forgotten how to do them by hand.

We ran out of the right kind of detergent.

It's our daughter's responsibility to do them tonight, and she's still out playing.

The vacuum cleaner fell apart and we can't afford to get it fixed.

We've just had a children's birthday party in here.

If I cleaned it up the kids would just mess it up all over again.

We're getting some new furniture tomorrow, so there's no point in cleaning until we get all this old stuff cleared out.

We plan to start painting this room tomorrow.

I'll get on that just as soon as I finish the bathroom and the bedroom.

We just returned and discovered that vandals have broken in.

Some unpleasant acquaintances were due to come over, so we left the place this way to encourage them to leave early.

Between the P.T.A., the Brownies, and my part-time job, I just don't have time to do proper housework.

I figure if I wait long enough, my husband will start appreciating all I do for him.

If it gets dirty enough, my family might start helping out a little.

Ever since I started going to that woman's rap group, I've realized that those boring household chores have been a waste of my human potential.

A love of disorder is a sign of the creative temperament.

I was brought up to be a fine, sensitive lady, not a drudge.

I'm trying to force my husband to leave me.

I've always depended on my wife to do that stuff and now that I'm living alone, I don't know where to begin. Would you care to give me a few pointers?

I'm an anal personality type in reverse.

I've been sick.

Let's wait till Spring.

CHAPTER *5*

Animals

❧ The trick here is to know your excusee. Is he or she one of those little old ladies who has found true love at last in the form of a Boston bull terrier or, instead, the type who bristles with allergies at the mere sight of fur or feathers and would just as soon see Fido as fertilizer?

Our Pets

My pedigreed Samoyed jumped the fence and ran off into the hills.

My hound ran the meter reader up the elm tree. There may be legal problems.

My poodle was attacked by the neighbor's mongrel. I've got to get her right to the vet.

Our A.K.C.-registered Irish setter is in the back yard about to get laid by a big stud dog we paid hard-earned cash to hire. We've got to watch them for the next two hours. Interested in a puppy cut-rate? (Make sure it's mating time.)

A dog with bloody sores at the end of its penis is chasing our spaniel all over the street.

I left my rod and reel in the garage and forgot to remove the hook, and Ginger snapped at it and got it stuck in her lip. It's a "trouble hook," impossible to remove without surgery. She is whimpering like hell and the kids are all upset, so it's off to the vet fast.

The cat slashed the dog in the eye and we're all out of methylene blue.

The nail of Fido's dewclaw is ingrown and maybe infected. I'm told I should rush him to the vet as it takes a "guillotine forceps" to slice the nail without crushing the end of the digit.

The dachshund can't climb up the front steps. We think she's displaced a vertebra, so we're taking her to the pet chiropractor to be elongated.

Our greyhound has the squirts and I've got to watch him constantly. Shall I bring him along to the drive-in?

Just as I was leaving, the puppy piddled all over my seersucker pants.

The boxer swallowed the car keys.

The spitz dragged the waterhose into the living room. The carpet is a disaster.

I won't be able to go hiking. I left my boots in the garage and our wolfhound tore them to shreds.

I can't spend the night with you because my dog is not used to staying at home all night by himself. He'd bark and cry and keep the neighbors awake. It's too late to take him to a kennel.

We have to go back home and feed the dog. If she misses a meal she goes crazy and tears up the garage.

Sorry, but the poodle has an appointment at the beauty parlor.

The retriever has been chewing the ivy again. Whenever that happens I'm supposed to discipline her by stuffing ivy into her mouth and taping it shut.

Tell them I'm not at home—I'm out walking the dog.

Our cat is stuck in a treetop.

The cat ran away. I couldn't enjoy myself at the party thinking he might have come home and, finding us absent, gone off again.

May Wong, our Siamese, is having her litter. In fact, she's eating up the third amniotic sac right now, and it looks like there's more to come. Do you want a cute kitten?

I have to go outside and break up a cat fight. Our old tom always gets creamed and ends up costing us thirty dollars for antibiotics.

The tabby had a hysterectomy.

I'm going back to the market for some fresh liver. My husband bought some Nine Lives, but our cat is a *very* fussy eater.

I'm late because the cat knocked the alarm-clock radio off the nightstand.

Would you care to come over and watch me drown five unwanted kittens?

Sorry, but Monday afternoon is the only time I have free to exercise my gelding.

The mare is foaling and it appears to be breached.

I was just notified that our horse is limping, so I've got to hurry over to the stable.

We're entering our Appaloosa at the country fair, but we may be disqualified if we don't keep applying poultices to his swollen ligament.

Frances, our nanny goat, has to be milked no later than six P.M. come hell or high water. Catch you at seven.

The electric filter on our aquarium broke down last night and the water has gone foul. I've got ninety dollars worth of blue tangs and tiger oscars in there, and five have already died. The kids are crying. I'll have to take that rig back to the pet shop for an exchange.

The aquarium is full of gas bubbles. We'll have to transfer the fish to neutral water.

My prize-winning guppy is having babies and I have to scoop them out before they get eaten up by the other fish.

The hamster is out of his cage and the cat is loose.

Some mean neighbor just poisoned our rabbit.

Our canary's nails have grown so long she can't hold onto her perch. We're about to do a clipping job.

My dog (or cat, horse, goat, rooster, fish, chameleon, etc.) died. He was quite old, a regular member of the family, and the wife and kids are all down in the dumps. Tomorrow I'll have to arrange for some kind of formal burial.

Other Creatures

A huge snarling great dane kept me from getting into my car.

Let's bug out of that dinner. I'm afraid of dogs and their pet bull terrier is a mean one that seems to hate my guts.

A puppy ran under my right front tire. Its owners, a couple of neighborhood kids, were blubbering with grief, so I had to comfort them and offer to pay for a burial and also a new pup. It was an awful mess!

I was in the park feeding Fritos to a squirrel and the damn thing bit my finger. I hear they're often rabid, so I rushed off to my doctor.

I went horseback riding and the nag threw me and ran off. I got lost trying to find my way back through the woods.

A rat is loose somewhere in our house. We're on a search-and-destroy mission.

A coyote has been trying to break into our chicken pen. Tonight I'm staking out with my twenty-two.

A rattlesnake came out of the fields and right now it's coiled up on my front sidewalk. I've called the fire department and I've got to stand guard until they arrive. What if some kid came walking by and didn't notice the thing? I might have a death on my conscience.

I took my in-laws out to Lion Country Safari and a tiger chewed up one of my tires.

Some seagulls flew over me and I had to go back home and change clothes.

Also Plants

My romaine lettuce is infested with aphids. Spray-can time.

The plant meal around my philodendron is dry as dust.

I have to tend to my victory garden before the weeds get a stranglehold on the tomato plants.

I bought these ash trees and drove them home in a truck, and now it looks as if they're wind-shocked. If I don't plant them fast and sock in plenty of vitamins, they'll be goners and I'll be out thirty bucks.

I'm in the middle of planting some pine trees in my parkway. The holes are dug, the earth is mulched, and the containers have already been sheared open. If I don't get these babies into the ground right away, and pack them in and wet them down, they'll all die of root exposure.

My neighbor complained that my big elm is shedding leaves into his swimming pool, so I promised to prune it on the weekend. And today is Saturday.

My back yard is full of toadstools and the dog keeps trying to eat them. It'll take me an hour to clear them out.

Some stray tom cat keeps peeing in our gardenia bed, and one of the plants is already dead. I've got to stand guard awhile and try to shoo the beast off.

Sorry, but tennis is out. Yesterday I spent four hours removing the stump of a thirty-year-old oak tree, and this morning I'm too stiff to walk.

Tonight I have to stay home and talk to my African violets.

CHAPTER **6**

Family and Friends

◄§ Because they offer revealing glimpses into our private lives, stories involving our friends and relatives usually catch an interested ear. If this doesn't happen, try adding spicier details.

Using Them

Frankly, I've been having a terrible hassle with my wife. It's been going on all week, and last night she slept in the den. If I came with you tonight I think she would move out for keeps. I was sure you'd understand.

For some time I've suspected my husband of meeting another woman after his bowling sessions. Since I can't afford to pay a private investigator, I have to keep tailing him myself.

Sorry to cancel out, but my husband is flying to Denver on business and I have to do some important last-minute errands for him.

My brother wrecked his car in Riverside. He might've been drinking, I'm not sure. Either way I have to pick him up and bring him back in time for work. It's serious since he's been absent so often lately that they're threatening to fire him.

I'm spending the evening with my sister. Her ex-husband keeps trying to break into her apartment, and she thinks my presence will discourage him.

I have to go camping with my parents. They don't like my staying home alone all weekend.

I'll be at my parents' the whole day. They're really hurt that I've bugged out the last three times they've asked me over. I even forgot to phone Mom on her birthday. Its time for the expiation.

Mom and Dad are getting married today.

My father won't let me.

This year we've agreed to spend Easter Sunday with her parents.

My Armenian uncle just flew in from Lebanon, and this is the only day he can spend with us because he has to go up to Fresno to see his nine brothers and forty-three nieces, nephews, and cousins.

A month ago I promised to join my folks at a dinner for Aunt Lurlene. She's the last member on the maternal side of my family—an honest-to-God ninety-four. Since Lurlene's developed a weird tumor in her bladder, there will probably never be a ninety-fifth, so this is the biggie, and I'd be a rat to bug out.

A couple of my old high school buddies called me up to remind me that Friday is the fifteenth annual reunion. I skipped the fifth and the tenth, so I'm locked into this one. It's going to be a stickily sentimental evening and probably a bore, but how could I beg off?

My old college roomie invited me to her baby shower.

Sorry I'm late. I went out shopping and who did I run into but my old girlfriend and her husband and two kids. I haven't seen her for eight years, so naturally we had a little on-the-spot reunion with lots of vague talk about getting together whenever they get back here or I got up to Jerkwaterville—which could be never.

Al, my old army buddy, is just in from Amarillo for a trade convention. I told him long ago that he had an open-end invitation to stay over anytime he came to town. Sorry it had to be this weekend. Bring him along? I'm afraid that wouldn't work—he's got a wife and three kids with him. Besides, he says he's bought a half-gallon jug of Wild Turkey and wants to sit up all night beating the gums about old times.

Instead of driving separately, I foolishly left my car and went along with my friends. Well, they insisted on staying an extra hour, so I was stuck, and on the way back they just had to stop off at a Howard Johnson's for coffee, which took up another half hour.

Eddie, my pal at work, has been in Alcoholics Anonymous for two years, and all of a sudden he thinks he is about to slide. For some reason he's afraid to tell his AA cronies and wants me to come by instead. Maybe I can talk some sense into him.

I have to take Don and Robbie to church. They're those blind kids. Their parents are paying me to drive them around.

I have to help Oscar move today. He has done me a lot of favors so now it's my turn to pitch in. Not that I'm looking forward to it; he has a big piano and he lives on the third floor. Would you care to lend a hand?

(Also see "Other People's Ailments," page 29.)

Excusing Them

Mary never smoked, drank, or cursed until she married that s.o.b.

He's not really sullen, he's just shy. If he got to know you he'd give you the shirt off his back.

That vicious punch on the shoulder is just his idea of a friendly greeting.

He thought you were a cop.

She didn't mean you in particular, she meant men in general.

He wasn't shining you on. He's just hard of hearing.

She ran out of tranquilizers.

Her constant nagging is just a form of affection.

He fell apart after his wife left him.

It's his job that has made him tense and suspicious. Unfortunately he's been working there for twenty-three years.

Try to overlook his beard, tattoos, and racing leathers and keep remembering that he was once a Rhodes scholar.

He only smokes pot because all his friends do.

Just because a guy has spent ten years in San Quentin doesn't make him all bad.

He grew up in Texas.

He's done nothing worse than wear silk nighties to bed. You've got to allow wealthy people their eccentricities.

I grant you they make a rotten couple, but they're wonderful when you meet them separately.

Just because she likes to flirt doesn't make her promiscuous. Of course if you're really interested, I'll pass the word along.

It's taken ten years but we've grown to like her—a little.

CHAPTER 7

The Job

◄§ Everybody respects "the job." It is more than bread and butter; it is the car we drive, the house we live in, the essence of our social status. And since it consumes most of our waking hours, constituting an impenetrable screen to all but our fellow workers (for whom some "On-the-Job Copouts" are provided), work is the catch-all of catch-alls, a massive riverhead of errands and duties and rituals that the excuse maker must learn to harness at all costs.

To Outsiders

I have to work overtime on Saturday morning. (Here and elsewhere, make sure that your excusee can't phone you or, worse, come by to visit you in the office. If possible, indicate that you won't be in your regular spot but instead out at the warehouse or at the other plant—and you're not sure which one.)

Not tonight, I'm afraid. I'm running an Au 6 purity analysis; also I have to have a Knoop hardness test completed for a customer and I'm doing some special environmental research that has to be wrapped up by the end of the week. (Substitute other baffling details from law, banking, engineering, marketing, etc.)

Our union has called an emergency meeting. We may have to go out on strike.

One of the men in the shop ran a drill into his hand. I saw it happen so I have to come in and review the accident report.

My boss just flew back East and I have to take over for him this week, so I'll be up all night studying his procedures manuals.

One of our managers was about to catch a flight to the home office in Chicago when he discovered he had forgotten to take some key contracts and blueprints. I had to race over to the airport with the stuff.

Ever since that jerk got to be a supervisor he's been acting like Hitler. For the third night in a row he's made us stay an extra hour, and we're not getting overtime for it.

Well, my performance review meeting lasted till way after quitting time, and then the boss asked me to join him for a toddy across the street. I think he's considering me for a promotion and wants to get to know me better. I couldn't very well refuse, now could I?

My boss has invited me over to his house to work out a strategy for Monday's meeting with the directors.

My boss is running for councilman and I had to go to a pre-election dinner downtown. The beef stroganoff was lousy and the speeches were worse.

My company has asked me to volunteer a couple of evenings a month to help out at the Braille Institute, and tonight is my turn. Actually I don't mind; it's a fascinating experience and good for mucho brownie points on the job.

They've started a new training course right in the plant. It runs from quitting time to seven. I guess I'll attend because it means three units of college credit plus a small salary increase.

I signed up with a part-time secretarial pool, which means I'm on call anytime for emergency jobs. And darned if they didn't call me just five minutes ago. No, I never know where they're sending me till I get to the pool.

Frankly, I'm so plumb exhausted from overwork that I'm just going to sack in for most of the weekend.

Occupational Specialties

The lawyer: There was a sudden change of venue.

The waiter: The owner threw a late private party for one of his suppliers.

The airline pilot: There was too much fog so we had to circle back to Tucson.

The trucker: I'm still on the dirty side grappling with the bear. (Really the beaver.)

The projectionist: They're running a midnight sneak preview.

The dentist: It was an emergency abscess.

The doctor: (a) She went into labor prematurely. (b) We forgot to take out the sponge when we sewed her up, so we're going back in. (c) I'd never get any rest if I didn't hide out in the desert on weekends. (d) I'm holding up until my malpractice insurance is reinstated.

The psychoanalyst: This one has a money-spending neurosis, so tonight we're in for a marathon session.

The college teacher: It's a week before final exams, and I still have two hundred term papers to correct.

The grade-school teacher: I'm scheduled for an after-school conference with an irate parent who thinks the new math is a communist plot.

The actor: We're behind schedule on those retakes, and my monster makeup takes four hours to assemble.

The "New Army" professional: The C.O. decided to throw a G.I. party for old time's sake. I got to man the mop.

The salesman: The whole deal hinged on my ability to beat him in an all-night backgammon game.

The aerospace engineer: We're competing with Boeing and

Lockheed, and our new proposal has to be submitted no later than nine A.M. tomorrow.

The politician: My former typist has been dating a snoopy reporter, so I have to drive some packets of hundred-dollar bills over to the laundry.

The reporter: I smell a story there, but I'll have to stake out patiently in the café across the street.

The private investigator: His wife got in the guy's car, but all they did was go to a porno movie. I sat behind them through two super features and finally had to rush out to the rest room. That's when I lost them.

The policeman: (a) I had to work undercover all night at a flophouse. (b) Twice I almost caught that van, and then it crossed over the state line. (c) It was a Code Three.

The barber: The last guy who came into the shop decided he wanted a shave, a massage, a shampoo, a style job, and a dye job.

The hooker: He wanted a two-hundred-dollar job.

On-the-Job Copouts

I swear I never received that new procedures memo. But then how would I with the screwed-up messenger service we have around here?

How could I write an update of that specification when the original is nowhere to be found? Somebody had better straighten out the company's archives.

I was going to finish that job first thing, but the supervisor told me to do something else.

I was helping a customer at the time.

One of my customers looked like he was having a heart attack. I called First Aid but their line was busy. Then I noticed that the man was leaving the store. I followed him out to try to help him, but he got away.

The loan officer who was handling your account quit last month.

Evidently there was a computer error.

This project will need lots of further study before we can give it the green light.

Our Xerox machine has broken down again. Had to run all over the plant looking for another one.

Those yo-yos in Stores gave me light steel, of all things. It takes forever to run that stuff.

That patient would have recovered if our emergency generators had been inspected properly before the power failure.

I can't help you. At the moment we are miserably understaffed, and it's all the fault of Personnel.

This Affirmative Action hiring policy is killing us. Whenever we try to fill a key spot, they send us unskilled dames and minorities. We can't train them because they're absent half the time.

I just can't work alongside that egg-sucking, chicken-stealing, anti-Semitic redneck bastard.

Our number-one problem is morale, and it's all on account of that back-stabber who calls himself our foreman.

Why I Lost My Job

I was overqualified. The job called for an AA degree, and when they found out I had a BA and realized they'd have to pay me more, they politely edged me out.

They merged with another division and my job classification was dropped.

They lost a big contract and had to let thirty of us go.

I was so quick to grasp the entire operation that the boss regarded me as a potential rival and never rested until he found a way to get me canned.

When I was hired they promised me a salaried position within a year, but they kept backing down. Finally I gave them an ultimatum.

They have a "no smoking" rule that they didn't tell me about when they hired me.

The superintendent's nineteen-year-old son got my job as a Christmas present.

That blonde I was meeting in the bar turned out to be my boss's wife.

That creep I worked with kept making cracks about my religion. Finally I had to punch him in the mouth.

I shouldn't have told the new foreperson that she ought to be home getting dinner ready for her husband.

I decided to use up some of my sick leave, and they sent a company spy over who claimed I was painting my house. Actually I was only wire-brushing it.

In that field you've got to kiss too many asses. I prefer to tell people what I really think of them—and often that ain't much.

To get to the top there you have to be a total conformist, a robot. There is no place for spontaneous, creative types like yours truly.

To make it you've got to play golf, and I can't.

To make it you've got to attend their cocktail parties, and I wouldn't.

To make it you've got to be one of "them," and I wasn't.

Deep down I guess I wanted out of that job. Why else would I have gone in an hour late every day and passed out left-wing propaganda and tried to seduce the boss's secretary? Thank God it's over!

CHAPTER *8*

The Official Summons

✑ It goes without saying that the single bright spot in encounters with the law or government is that they make terrific excuses.

Cops

I was pulled over for a highway safety check. I got tagged for a misaligned headlight.

He stopped me because I drive a Porsche. They all do.

Since my car has small tires and is lowered in the back, they really checked me over for contraband.

I saw the vehicle inspection up ahead and, in trying to avoid it, turned into a weird curved street and got lost for fifteen minutes.

He followed me for three miles, so I had to go fifty-five. Then he stopped me and said my muffler was too loud and cited me. Grrr!

I got caught doing 21½ miles per hour in that speed trap.

I was flagged over for going too slow on the freeway. I explained to the patrolman that I was getting an odd vibration in the engine and didn't want to push it, but he chastised me anyway. Luckily no ticket.

My buddies and I were coming home from the ball game when the car got smashed into by a drunk. Nobody was hurt on our end, but we had to wait for the cops, an ambulance, and a fire truck and then talk to all of them until 1:30 A.M.

As I was trying to jimmy open my front window, two squad cars came roaring up, and in no time I was in handcuffs and being transported to the local constabulary. That'll teach me to leave my keys and wallet in the china cabinet.

I was pulled over and questioned because a car just like mine had been used in a liquor-store holdup.

They're after me for seven parking tickets.

I was bowling and drinking beer all evening, and on the way home I stopped at a vacant lot to relieve myself behind a bush. And whataya know, a cop pulls up and busts me for indecent exposure.

I borrowed a friend's van to load up some of my old furniture for the mountain cabin, and some old lady across the street reported me as a burglar.

The officer thought my prosthetic hook was a gun.

He mistook me for some other hooker.

He was one of those moron country cops, the ones that didn't have the smarts to pass the test for the city force.

Because of my dark complexion and the crucifix I wear on my necklace, they're always questioning me as an illegal alien.

Some shoplifter, sensing that she was being followed out to the parking lot, dropped ten lobster tails into the back of my pickup. They're holding me instead.

I was twenty minutes late returning my daughter from our Sunday outing, and my ex-wife reported me as a kidnapper.

I never realized that my collection of old submachine guns could get me into trouble.

The police have apparently gotten me mixed up with another Jacob Vernon Cushman, but in the meantime they're searching my apartment for a bloodstained ice pick and making all kinds of urgent phone calls. This could go on all night. Incidentally, will you call my lawyer?

Listen, those guys started the fight.

(Also see Chapter 17, "To the Traffic Cop.")

Courts, Etc.

I have to testify in court.

While this is an unassailable excuse, it is advisable to know the precise location of the courthouse and to have some specific details on the offense you have witnessed. Some routine examples:

I saw a guy running out of a drugstore waving a gun. They caught him with twelve bucks.

A man was beating up on his wife in front of a bar and grill.

A woman was trying to hit her little boy with a poker.

An old codger was exposing himself to a busload of nuns.

I bought some stolen tee-shirts at a swap meet. (It's probably not important to know how the case finally turned out.)

This is the day I take my former tenant to the small-claims court for the expensive mattress he defiled in unspeakable ways.

This is the day I sock it to my former landloard for the cleaning deposit he never returned.

All I called her was a crazy whore, and the crazy whore is suing me for slander.

I have to make an appearance at the court house to get excused from jury duty.

I've decided that it's my duty as a citizen to serve on that jury after all.

Today my best friend is being naturalized as a U.S. citizen. I've promised to be there as a witness.

I know the war is over, but Selective Service apparently lost my records, and now the Army Department has me mixed up with some deserter who ran off to Guatemala. If I don't get this straightened out, I may end up cleaning bedpans for the next two years.

My IRS audit comes up tomorrow, and I'm going nuts trying to dig out last year's receipts and check stubs. It'll probably tie me up all night.

Other Pressing Matters

Tonight I have to do some last-minute cramming for my civil service exam.

That civil service exam is today.

I've been thinking about switching jobs. I sent a trial application to one place and whataya know, they want to interview me right away.

I just realized my auto insurance has run out. If I can catch my agent before three P.M., he'll be able to reinstate my policy.

My cleaning woman says she won't come back until I set up a Workman's Compensation policy for her. Where do I go for one?

My ex-wife claims I'm delinquent on the child-support payments, so I've been called over to her lawyer's office. It's got to be today or I could wind up back in court.

Since they've reactivated the G.I. housing loan program, I've been considering a move out to that swell new beach suburb. Consequently I have to go over to the Veterans Administration and show them my discharge and get a new file started. And today's the day.

We've been trying to sell our house since last May. Well, yesterday the realtor stopped by to show the place to a family, and ten minutes after they left I got a call that there was an offer. The problem is, I have to be present when the bid is officially made, and that's due to occur sometime this afternoon. I'll fill you in on the details later.

CHAPTER *9*

Weather and Acts of God

Rain

I didn't come over to play tennis because it's raining out our way and I figured the courts would be too slippery.

I stepped in a puddle and had to go back and change my shoes.

My car hydroplaned right off the road.

When I swung off the freeway, the surface street was flooded two feet deep. My car is still stuck there; I practically had to swim to this pay telephone.

The slope at the edge of our yard has turned into a big slithering mudslide. I'm trying to shore it up before it reaches the house.

There's a big crack in our wall at floor level, and our new carpet is half soaked. We'll be busy pulling out tacks.

There's no rain gutter on the back of the house, and all night long big drops of water kept pounding on the kid's wagon like drumbeats. It was too wet to go outside, so I kept my head under my pillow, but I never really got much sleep. This morning I'm a nervous wreck.

Are we overdue on that payment? We had a leak in our mailbox and all our bills were soaked to mush.

I caught a cold.

Ice and Snow

I left my car out all night and now it's buried in four feet of snow. The city will have to dig it out. In the meantime I'll start hitchhiking.

Our house will probably be buried till April, so we'll be calling you from California.

I can only find one snowshoe.

I took my gloves off to light a cigarette and my hands got so totally numb that I had to go back home and warm them over the radiator.

We forgot to bring our arctic gear.

While we were asleep in the motel, somebody stole our tire chains.

The water pipes are frozen.

The ignition is frozen and I can't turn the key.

As I was walking out the front door, a five-pound chunk of ice fell from the eaves and knocked me cold.

Fog

The coastal fog was so mushy I couldn't drive faster than ten miles per hour—not after witnessing that bloody head-on collision.

Our plane was grounded on account of zero visibility.

I've had a fog phobia ever since I saw that movie about Jack the Ripper.

Lightning

A big bolt hit the telephone pole out back and set it on fire. We were terrified that some high-voltage wires would start flying around and spread the juice.

It struck and killed a dog in front of our house, and right now we're all too spooked to set foot outdoors until the storm passes.

I think lightning is pretty. I want to stay home and watch it.

Wind

The wind blew our elm tree over and it landed on the dog house. Our cocker isn't really hurt, but she has gone into hysterics. I'm afraid she might attack the baby.

My redwood fence was blown over and my neighbor's geese got into my yard and are now running wild in the street. I guess I'm obligated to help him round them up.

The front window just landed on our Sunday dinner.

Our motor home was blown off the highway. We had to call a cab and spend the night in a six-dollar motel and eat Big Macs instead of your lovely chicken.

It wasn't much as twisters go, but it had enough pizazz to lob our gazebo into the drainage canal a block away.

The water will be much too rough for boating. Besides, I get seasick.

The updraft was so fierce it carried me and my hang-glider all the way into the next county.

Power Failure

Our alarm clock lost three hours.

I can't finish the pruning until the electric chain saw comes back on.

We just put five pounds of beef on the electric barbecue. I've got to rush out and buy some charcoal briquettes.

I was groping in the dark for some candles and I dislodged a ten-pound sack of flour. It landed by my back, and for the past ten minutes I haven't been able to unbend from a low crouch.

I think the sudden change in temperature is killing all our tropical fish.

The movie was interrupted for forty-five minutes. But we had a lot of fun sitting there in the dark.

Sorry I couldn't reach you, but the telephone lines were out.

Heat

My phonograph records are starting to curl. I'll have to put them in the car and drive around with the air conditioner on.

My denture glue keeps melting.

I even sweat when I'm in the shower. I'd hate to come to you unclean.

I couldn't meet your friends with heat prickles.

I got halfway up the mountain when my engine vapor locked.

I was digging out a fine chuck of raw jade when suddenly I keeled over into the sand. The next thing I knew I was lying on a cot in Palm Desert Hospital.

We'd love to come over and try out your new sauna. Maybe next February.

Humidity

The front door was swollen so tight we couldn't get out of the house.

The dinner table came apart at the joints and the tureen started sliding.

My energy level nosedives in all this humidity. Apologize for me to the rest of the crew.

Earthquake

Some psychic predicted eight points on the Richter scale for two P.M. today. We're staying under our doorjambs until at least 2:45.

There are bound to be aftershocks, so we would prefer not to drive into the city.

Our best crystal spilled out of the cabinet. It took us an hour to sweep up all the splinters.

I've got to check all the water pipes for ruptures.

My neighbor's house is teetering on the hillside. I have to get over there with my winch.

Other

A footbal-sized meteorite tore through the roof, brushed by the edge of our bed, and plunged three feet into the floor. We're moving out for the rest of the week.

PART TWO

SPECIAL PROBLEMS

If the Catch-Alls were as inclusive as they might seem at first glance, then this book would be all over. However, the real challenge is not one of typical situations but rather one of nuances—of sensitively sizing up each occasion in terms of its human ingredients, its present purpose, and its foreseeable aftereffects.

The special problems which follow ought to take you a long way toward finding the right note to strike, but even then your excuses will only be as good as your ability to sock them in.

CHAPTER *10*

Male and Female

Why You Shuold Go Out with Me

What began with Eve and the apple is ever beginning. At least one third of the world's songs and poems have been dedicated to the proposition, not to mention all the self-help manuals spanning the centuries from Ovid's *The Art of Love* to the recent *How to Pick Up Men*.

The core message of all these works is perhaps best summed up by the Roman poet Catullus:

> *Come, Lesbia, let us live and love*
> *nor give a damn what sour old men say.*
> *The sun that sets may rise again*
> *but when our light has sunk into the earth,*
> *it is gone forever.**

While later adapters of this classical "seize the day" theme (Shakespeare, Herrick, Marvell and a thousand more) seem to have been driven to outshine one another in fancy imagery or argumentation, there is still no good reason to laugh at the teenager making his game little pitch on the bedroom telephone. Mere cleverness

* From *The Poems of Catullus*, translated and with an Introduction by Horace Gregory. Copyright © 1956 by Horace Gregory. Reprinted by permission of Grove Press, Inc.

never won anybody's affections. In fact, many authorities in this matter claim that the most surefire approach is the one taken in that single-minded song refrain, "I'll give you a real good time." And sometimes it is wisest to keep one's mouth shut and let the eyes say it.

Or to try apples.

TIMID

Since Jerry will be out of town, I figured you might let me take you to the square dance instead. Just thought I'd ask.

I just happen to have an extra ticket for the basketball game, and—well—er—

There's a dynamite double feature at the Fox. Good popcorn too.

It looks like a super day for a picnic.

Have you been to the Starburst? They make real good boogie there.

I can borrow my brother's Porsche. It has stereo.

I can teach you to water ski free of charge.

I'm doing a photo essay on the railroad yard, and I need someone to stand in front of the engines to give them scale, preferably someone—ah—pretty like you. Naturally I'll buy you lunch for your trouble.

You look like you could use a good meal, and my dolmades are the world's greatest.

I'm redecorating my apartment, and I could sure use some feminine advice.

You look big and strong. Do you think you could come over and help me move my sofa across the living room?

They've been laughing at me ever since she ran off with the

meter reader. I just want you to hang around awhile and help me save face.

You may not remember me, but I sat behind you in homeroom.

You can't imagine how long it's been since I met someone I can really talk to on an intelligent level.

You mean to say you're as crazy about Olivia Newton-John as I am?

You score eight points on a ten-point compatibility test I just read in *McCall's*.

I have a feeling that you and I could get along beautifully.

It's been fifteen months since you went into mourning.

You have very expressive eyes.

You have wonderful feet, and I'm crazy about those ankle-straps on your high-heeled shoes.

Your sister is a very good friend of my sister.

Daddy approves of you.

You remind me of my mother.

I like you.

RIGHT-ON
I think I love you.

I've been searching for you for ten years, and I'm not about to lose you after a five-minute cup of coffee.

It's too smoky in here. Join me in a stroll to the back bedroom?

Mine is an open marriage.

I'll put it to you bluntly: My husband is stationed in Germany and my boyfriend has been serving ninety days for the last sixty.

Latin types have been my downfall. My therapist thinks I should try a Scandinavian for a while.

Two years in analysis haven't cured my frigidity, but I just know I could make it with the right person.

Help me! Help me! I don't want to go on living with that dyke!

I've had it with massage parlors.

Some night you'll get tired of playing mah-jongg with that old dude, and you know I'll be on tap.

Why don't you stop fooling around with punk kids and try a real man for a change?

I want to do certain strange things to you.

I know you want to do strange things. I don't mind at all.

You've got to use it or you'll lose it.

Have you ever tried it with coke?

Have you ever tried it the Zambian way?

I just bought that ointment they advertise in *Penthouse*. Give me another chance.

The doctor gave me one gram of Probenecid and 3.5 of Ampicillin. I'm fine now.

I may not look like much, but I can show you some great testimonials.

You'll never notice my hand-sized purple birthmark in the dark.

If you knew what you were passing up, you would slash your wrists.

Let's you and me get it on.

Why I Can't Go Out with You

Amour calls for great self-awareness. Once you have decided not to go out, is your admirer the live one whom you would really like to go on seeing, the so-so commodity whom you have no good reason to alienate, or that schnook who ought to vanish into thin air? Or any of those grayer things in between?

To aid you in your maneuvering, we have subdivided our rejections into the smooth, the neutral, and the rough ones. We thought about trying a further classification into excuses that are checkable versus those that are foolproof, but that seemed impossible. Nobody is more persistent in ferreting out the truth than an ardent, jealous suitor. He or she will call or visit you at the office, classroom, and hospital, and in times of stress is not above tailing your car or peeking through your window at midnight.

SMOOTH

Please don't get mad at me, but all the guys are going down to Juarez and I've never been there before and I've wanted to go. If you say no I won't. I promise to bring you back a fifth of tequila and take you someplace extra nice next weekend.

The final notice on my car payments came, and I had to send the dough off right away. Frankly, I hate to take *you* out unless I can do it up big. Can't we wait till next Saturday?

My boss just called to tell me that the guy on swing shift can't make it in to work, so I'm going to have to fill in for him just for tonight. Look at it this way, it's more money for next weekend. Yeah, I'm sorry too.

I'll be honest—I've got to see Andy tonight. You know, the fellow I broke up with when I met you. I tried so hard not to hurt him, but he seems to be taking the whole thing very badly. He even sounds a bit suicidal. Let's see if I can't talk some sense into him.

Going to the luau with you would be heavenly, but Fred asked me earlier and I said I wasn't going at all because I didn't want to go with *him*. Still, I don't want him to think I'm a liar. Listen, I won't mind a bit if you take Sue instead. (Sue is your ugliest friend.)

I'd love to go with you, but that wimp Ron asked me out and I can't break it because he's my dad's best friend's son. I'll be thinking of you in my misery.

My little brother has the flu and I don't want to take a chance of passing it on to you. Let's wait a couple of days.

My ex-husband just got out of jail and he's been phoning me. He's a mean, vindictive type—also a former welterweight fighter— and I'm afraid to take a chance on our running into him. Especially for your sake.

THE TELEPHONE DODGE

Start by phoning to confirm the date. After a few moments of pleasant chatter, have your little sister call out to you in a loud voice. Beg to be excused, then soon return in an agitated state to tell her that you can't make it after all because you've got to drive across town to assist your father who is stranded on a freeway overpass with a blown-out water pump.

NEUTRAL

Not just now. I'll let you know when.

I completely forgot that tonight is my night to cook for the family.

This would be a bad night for you to come by. My mom and dad will be in the living room playing bridge with their friends, and they need me to serve the iced tea.

I can't go out to dinner with you because my parents insist that I go out with them. The usual deal.

My grandmother, aunt, uncle, and three nieces just dropped in and it doesn't look like they will be leaving for hours. Come on over if you can stand it.

I had insomnia last night—couldn't doze off till four A.M. Now I'm just too tired to do anything but sleep.

Believe it or not, I don't have any underwear left, so I've got to do my laundry.

I thought I had an extra week to do my research paper, but it turns out it's due *this* Monday. I guess I'll be burning the midnight oil.

Tonight I have to watch the Cousteau special for Zoology (or the heart-attack special for Health Education, the Benjamin Franklin special for History 1A, the Antonioni movie for Survey of Films, etc.).

Sorry I forgot that I'm registering for night classes. I'll probably have to take the placement test.

How can I go with a sprained ankle?

I've got terrible cramps.

I just put my hair up in rollers.

I went to my hairdresser's for a color rinse and he used the wrong stuff and my hair has turned a weird kind of orange. I'm ashamed to see anybody until I get back over there on Monday to have it straightened out.

I'll have to say indoors for a while. You know how blah I've been feeling—well, my doctor thinks it's mononucleosis. They call that the kissing disease.

My wife has been acting suspicious. Let's cool it for a few days.

I have to rise at the crack of dawn to get my bike in shape for the race at the speedway.

Gee, I don't know if I can on Friday. It seems like there's something I have to do, but I can't remember what it is. I'll talk to Debbie to make sure and you call me back on Thursday so I can let you know one way or the other. I might be able to go, but I hate to say yes without knowing for sure.

My mom has been in a rotten mood all day and she started yelling at me for going out too much. She is making me stay home every night this week.

There must be some misunderstanding. Our date was last night and you didn't show up.

ROUGH

After giving it careful consideration, I just don't think it can ever work out between us.

Maybe sometime, if you'll take me to a John Travolta movie. He's my fantasy male.

I'd rather stay home and watch *Three's Company* with my sisters.

My parents are scared to death of your new carpeted van—and so am I.

I might be interested if you would bathe regularly and shave off that silly-looking mustache.

Whatever you spray your hair with gives me skin prickles.

I'll have to cancel out. My date with Mary is on again after all.

I've got the swine flu. Why don't you come over?

I'd love to go there, but not with you.

The word is out that you're a real drag.

My big brother says he'll bash your teeth in if he ever sees you again.

Me go to McDonald's in that beat-up El Camino? Listen, I've had my fill of losers.

Not until you show your worth by performing some heroic deed—like driving onto the "Wrong Way" lane.

You're flabby, my dear.

Avoiding the Invitation

I got engaged last weekend.

You know, I feel just like a sister to you.

I make it a firm policy never to date a guy who is in one of my classes (or who is over thirty or under twenty or a co-worker, a Catholic, a divorcee, a wine drinker, a smoker, etc., etc.).

I'm sorry, you're a Scorpio.

Right now I'm part of an experimental control group. I've made a pledge to a certain dating service to go out only with people they've referred to me on the basis of their computer-scored psychological tests.

I'm on an independence kick. I do what I want *when* I want, and there is no telling where I'll be at any given time.

Dampening the Proposition

I've have to know you a lot better.

I've got to be in love or it's no go.

Not until I get through the next phase of my therapy—the part where we get into the origin of my frigidity.

Tonight I have to give my undivided attention to my pillow speaker.

My husband has promised to take me back on a probationary basis, so one slipup and I'm finished.

My boyfriend refuses to sleep three in a bed.

I've been menstruating steadily for three weeks.

I've got the clap.

My wife is ovulating and she wants to get pregnant this time. First things first.

You're an ambitious little tyke, aren't you.

Sir, you have tiny hands and tiny feet.

Hey, knock it off!

(After a long, searching appraisal of the merchandise) I'm sorry, honey, but you just won't do.

Love As An Excuse

Guys, I got a call from this chick I knew in high school. She had just gotten back in town and she wanted to see me. Well, I remembered her as being kind of wimpy but nice, so what the hell, I agreed to buy her a cup of coffee. Now when I went over to pick her up, can you believe what a fantastic change had taken place? I mean suddenly she's the fox and I'm the one that's doing all the work. So if you don't hear from me for a week or two, you'll know what I'm into.

What a party! This morning I woke up in bed with the wrong woman in the wrong bedroom. When I got out, my car was nowhere to be found, so I had to hitchhike back, and in my stocking feet.

When I tried to put my arms around her, she tossed me right off the front porch. I pegged her as one of those libber self-defense freaks and decided not to argue the point. So you can imagine how surprised I was yesterday when she called and asked me to come over and spend the night as her roommate was gone for the week. I came prepared, and then her shenannigans started up again—this time a couple of swift elbow-jabs in my ribs. It took us till three in the morning to finally come to terms. I guess it was worth it despite the bruises. Anyway, I just walked in the door when you called, and I'm so pooped out I think I'll sack in all day. I'd better, since I'm seeing her again tonight.

Sorry I couldn't make it last night. Larry, my old college flame, called to ask me out for one little drink. Well, that martini hit him pretty hard because he started proposing all over again. It took me two hours to cool him down.

Not that I want to get married, but I think George is really going to ask me this evening, and I wouldn't miss that spiel for anything.

I know he is shy and ineffectual, but right after he said good-night and started shuffling away I heard him murmur "I love you." At least I think that's what he said. Anyway, I just had to ask him in.

He may be a goy but he is tall, blond, beautiful, and just starting his internship at Cedars-Sinai Hospital. I don't know where I'll be next weekend—it's all up to him.

I just met her—Miss Wonderful! Zap! Where's that great French restaurant you were telling me about? And can you loan me fifty bucks till Friday?

Listen, I just want to be alone with my chick.

Why I Didn't Make Out

I didn't dare try, knowing my underware was stained.

I shouldn't have eaten all that garlic bread.

Her parents arrived home unexpectedly.

Her little brother kept peeking in.

Her husband has decided that he wants her back.

I couldn't get it up when she told me about her fiancé's black belt in karate.

She says she can't trust me after hearing about my reputation as a swinger.

That dumb political argument we had spoiled everything.

I think I'm in love with her and don't want to get the relationship on a sex basis until I've sorted it all out.

I think I'm not in love with her and don't want to get too deep into something I may want to get right out of.

I forgot that it was her birthday.

She thinks I smoke too much.

I'm a skin freak, and she has weird moles.

She turned out to be the motherly type.

She was too aggressive. I like to make the advances.

I found her sister more attractive.

Performance Problems

Call it shyness, but I'm always this way the very first time, especially with someone I really like.

I hurt my back lifting heavy crates.

I got caught in my zipper.

The trouble is that pitcher of beer I drank with my pizza. Where's the john?

But you said there would be a closed-circuit porno movie.

Why aren't you wearing that blond wig and black nightie I bought you?

Water beds make me nauseous.

I slip and slide on satin sheets.

You should have shaved and showered.

Haven't you forgotten something?

My time is six days off—or is it seven—or eight? Do you think we'll be safe?

Believe me, it will make your headache go away.

I find it impossible when we've been arguing. Let's just hold hands and talk awhile about nice things.

I've got that tax audit on my mind.

I'm always impotent for a week after I run into my ex-wife.

I have to go by the book, and somebody stole my *Kama Sutra*.

I guess I'm just out of practice.

Now you know why my nickname is "Bunny."

Tell me you love me.

Why Our Evening Bombed

With a title like "Last Tango in Paris," you'd figure it would have been Gene Kelly and Cyd Charisse.

It just isn't Bogdanovich's kind of picture. Give him another try.

That play won four Tonys and ran two years on Off-Broadway. The trouble here is the out-of-town cast.

The *Miami Herald* loved it.

I didn't mind not being able to see the stage. It gave me a chance to really concentrate on the dialogue.

At ten dollars a head for closed-circuit TV, you'd have figured Ali to carry it at least three rounds!

I was sure you would love a good cockfight once you got into the spirit of the thing.

I couldn't refuse the free tickets.

I admit it was lousy Cantonese duck. Hung Fat used to make the best in town, but I just learned that they've changed their management three times since my last visit.

My dumb brother-in-law recommended this as the world's greatest steak house!

Hell, the waitress just had a bad day. It can happen.

Nobody told me there was an hour-and-a-half wait on Friday night.

Nobody told me you needed reservations.

I thought everybody honored BankAmericard.

We had the slow cooker filled with beef and all the other ingredients, and I plugged in the toaster instead.

Those steaks wouldn't have burned if you hadn't made me talk to your mother on the telephone.

I guess I should have told you that dancing, drinking, and smoking are against my religion.

I should never have switched to martinis.

How could I know that my transmission was going to fall out?

They forced me to bring my little brother along.

Why I Forgot Valentine's Day, Your Birthday, Our Anniversary, Etc.

The moment it dawns on you that you have forgotten, ask her if they have arrived—the two dozen longstemmed roses you ordered from an uptown florist. When she says they haven't, go to the telephone and dial the florist (any blind number will do) and angrily tell him off for getting the delivery date wrong. End the call with, "It was supposed to be a surprise. Since you blew my surprise, I'm cancelling the order." Take her out to an expensive restaurant instead.

Or—forgetting the whole florist turn—just say that her gift, meant to be a big surprise, is that fancy dinner.

Also:
I didn't forget, but you've been acting so sensitive about your age lately that I thought it would be discreet not to remind you you're a year older.

An hour ago I was in the kitchen looking for a beer and I noticed the new Rival Crock Pot—the one Aunt Jane gave us for Christmas. Well, you know, I'd completely forgotten about it and had gone out and bought you one of those for your birthday. So, realizing my error, I hurried back to the store to exchange it for something else. What I finally picked out was an item I'm sure you want and don't have, but the right model is out of stock until next Monday. Let's keep it a surprise until then, okay?

I'm buying you a super new outfit at the best boutique. The only problem is, whenever I've tried to buy you clothes before they've always been the wrong size or the wrong color. So this time I've decided to play it smart by taking you along and having you make the selection. The shop doesn't close till nine, so we've got plenty of time.

But our anniversary isn't until tomorrow, the twenty-third! (Insist on this, even to the point of whipping out the marriage license. Then offer to drive back to your office for that gift you swear you've been hiding in the desk. And hope she says it can wait till tomorrow.)

I thought we agreed to celebrate our anniversary on the date of our first kiss.

I had to leave your present to be gift wrapped and, when I returned, the store had already closed.

The wrappers gave me the wrong package. I noticed because it weighed ten pounds and what I bought you was a piece of jewelry. They're still conducting a search and promise to call me when they locate it.

This is my gift: all my love and a determination to be a better, kinder, and more understanding spouse in the days to come.

Valentine's Day means sweets, and I thought the sweetest thing of all would be a shower together and an early lurch for the sack.

A good general rule: Always keep at least one well-hidden all-purpose wrapped gift on hand for emergencies.

Why We Got Together

HE

I was just back from my two-year hitch in the Aleutians.

I loved the way she poured a can of beer.

She was the fastest typist I ever hired.

She said she shared my enthusiasm for restoring old Nashes.

She promised never to try to reform me. In fact she drinks more than I do.

She was the only girl I ever met who thought my weird habits were amusing.

She was the only one short enough for me.

She caught me on the rebound from Sylvia Blodgett.

She reminded me of Debra Paget in "Bird of Paradise."

She was the only one my parents ever approved of.

Her father promised me this good job if I would.

Her father promised me a load of shot in my belly if I didn't.

We got caught in an elevator together during the big blackout.

It took me too long to get the money together for the abortion.

It wasn't until she showed me the baby and I could see he had my nose and red hair that I finally consented.

She swore she would slash her wrists if I didn't.

She chased me so long and hard that I felt she had earned it.

She made an oath to lose thirty pounds.

She says I swept her off her feet.

She actually thought I was handsome.

I was always a sucker for redheads.

She smelled good.

I'm a boob man, and she sure qualified.

Her smile killed me.

I could never keep my feet warm in bed.

My tax accountant advised it.

I flipped a coin.

I was too drunk to know what I was doing.

SHE

I asked him to give me a back rub on the beach, and I liked the aggressive way he unfastened my bra.

He always ordered my favorite wine—bottles and bottles of it.

He sent me longstemmed roses on my birthday.

He wrote a dumb little poem.

He wore Musk aftershave.

He drove a TR-6.

He was the only one tall enough for me.

He was as big as an ox, and I liked being crushed.

He claimed he had a genius IQ.

He got promoted to senior clerk.

He inherited a house.

He said we would live in Paris. It turned out to be Paris, Arkansas.

He said he shared my enthusiasm for découpage.

He caught me on the rebound from Karl L. Shuster.

He reminded me of John Garfield in "Dust Be My Destiny."

All our friends were doing it.

I had nothing else to do that weekend.

He was my third and last try with the computer dating service, and I didn't want to see my money go down the drain.

He agreed with me that we should wait. Then I got tired of waiting.

It happened the night we watched "Love Story" together on the *Late Show*.

My therapist thought the sacred vows might help me to overcome my hostility.

My doctor thought I was superbly equipped for motherhood.

He said he wanted kids.

He had a violent streak, and I was afraid to refuse.

He swore he would blow his brains out if I didn't.

I could never bear to watch a man cry.

We had been living together for five years and there was nothing about him that absolutely disgusted me.

After a long struggle on my part, he finally swept me off my feet.

He passed the blood test.

He threatened to go back to Sylvia Blodgett.

He was my gynecologist.

Why We Split Up

HE

I thought I was dating an Audrey Hepburn until she took off her girdle and blossomed into Maureen Stapleton.

I thought she was thirty until she invited me to her grandson's bar mitzvah.

She would pile a can of mushrooms on the scrambled eggs and call that classy cooking.

I got tired of the Colonel's ribs night after night.

She refused to learn English.

For five years we never communicated without her analyst sitting between us.

She invited her widowed mother to move into our guest room.

It turned into a triangle: me, her, and Robert Redford.

She liked my buddies too much.

She always waited until we were in bed together to tell me about the kids' day at school and her plans for tomorrow's dinner.

She resented my superior intelligence.

She was always slugging me.

She couldn't get aroused unless I beat her up.

She had poor character. All she wanted to do was lie around and make love all day.

She passed her bar exam and started earning twice my salary.

She told all her friends about my bedwetting.

She got arrested for soliciting.

Imagine my shock at discovering that she wasn't a natural blonde!

I busted my ass for her at that shoeshine parlor, but she was never satisfied. Money money money!

She became a Jehovah's Witness.

She started wearing my clothes.

Somebody loaned her a copy of *Sexual Politics*.

SHE

He was always making excuses.

He wanted me to scrub his back the way his little old mother did.

My married name would have been Lupe Dupey.

He got me pregnant and moved back to Cincinnatti.

He was only interested in one thing.

He was only interested once a month.

He was more interested in Jack Daniels.

I got tired of wearing gloves, garter belts, and spiked heels.

He snored like a howitzer.

He stopped playing handball and gained seventy pounds.

I thought he was breeding horses, not betting on them.

When he said he was in the numbers game, I thought he was a C.P.A.

He got promoted to a high-paid construction job in Uganda.

He hired the babysitter to come sit with him.

He sold a script to Paramount and started chasing starlets around the Polo Lounge patio.

He pronounced Crown Russe "Roo-say."

His co-workers will tell you that he is the nicest guy in the world, but they're the only ones who ever saw him sober.

He said nasty things to my daddy.

His parents never got over his marrying a shiksa.

His idea of a great gourmet meal was Howard Johnson's weekly clam fry.

In fifteen years he never bought me a single bouquet of flowers.

He resented my going back to work at the massage parlor.

He wanted to raise our kids as Buddhists.

He went on welfare and I got tired of looking at him all day.

He spent our savings on a transsexual operation.

He quit his good job in the laundry and decided to become an actor.

He refused to see a marriage counselor—and so did I.

All our friends were splitting up.

We found it was cheaper than filing a joint return.

Somebody loaned him a copy of *The Manipulated Man*.

CHAPTER *11*

Money

Why I Can't Lend You Any

It's not the money, it's the principle of the thing.

Do you think it grows on trees?

Sorry, but I don't approve of the way you would spend it.

I leave all the financial decisions to my spouse.

If you need it so badly, how come you're driving a BMW while I'm still clunking around in that Rambler Rebel?

You earn half of it and I'll be glad to lend you the other half.

I'd rather not after what happened with Chuck, who used to be my friend. He borrowed fifty dollars from me and then couldn't pay it back right away. Well, I wasn't in any rush, but he seemed to think I was pressuring him and he dumped his anxiety right back on me by badmouthing me to other people. He finally paid me, but we've never been able to look each other in the eye since.

I just tied up every loose cent in a tax-sheltered savings account. I'm so close to going into a higher bracket that any withdrawal over twenty bucks will cause me to lose five hundred on my yearly refund.

With inflation the way it is, by the time you pay me back it will be worth only half as much.

My son is starting piano lessons next week, and it's been hell raising the tuition money. In fact, I was going to hit you for a ten-spot to cover the sheet music.

Sure, if you'll let me have your quadrasonic stereo as collateral.

I'll be happy to refer you to an excellent loan company.

First find a co-signer and then maybe we'll talk about it.

Sorry, but I couldn't be your co-signer. My own credit is so rotten I can't even buy a new toaster on time.

In the words of our Governor, we're all moving into an era of limited expectations. Try to do without.

You mean on top of the five dollars I've already loaned you?

Why I Can't Pay You Back

What five dollars?

I forgot my checkbook.

Nobody will cash my government check.

I was mugged and robbed in the park.

My furniture was repossessed, and I kept my savings in the mattress.

I thought you said you would give me until the first of the month, so I paid someone else off yesterday.

You should have asked me on Friday. I got paid, but then a buddy of mine got arrested for drunk driving and I was the only person he could contact for the bail money. It cleaned me out down to my last nickel. Catch me next Friday.

All I've got is one dollar and forty-three cents, but I insist that you take it.

Can you hold off for a few days? I just got a nasty letter from my chiropractor's collection agency. It was really a surprise to me.

The yearly premium on my automobile insurance just gobbled up my whole paycheck.

Our payroll computer's gone crazy again. Would you believe that my check came to a total of twenty-seven cents? It'll take them a couple of days to get it straightened out.

That flaky company I work for—their paycheck bounced! I can't even pay my rent.

Hey, I sent you your money! You never got it? That's impossible, things hardly ever get lost in the mail. Hmm, it probably got misfiled. You'd better tell your mailman to make a search. And keep checking with him. (This one is good for more stalling time as you must contact your bank to have that lost check voided.)

It's been six weeks since I mailed in my tax forms. The return check is due any minute now.

The IRS has made a terrible mistake on my refund.

That extra money I expected from the VA came in, but my file is so screwed up I don't dare spend it because I may have to send some of it back.

My only assets are my Planters Peanut stocks, and my broker advises me to wait another week before selling.

I'm practically broke and I've got to buy my mother a birthday present and my car is being repossessed. As a matter of fact, I could use another tenner just to make it through the week, but I wouldn't dream of asking you—you've been too generous already.

I can't return that fifty because I still haven't heard from the insurance company of the girl who rear-ended me on Hill Street. I was at a complete stop with my brakelights on and my right-turn signal flashing when she came out of nowhere in her yellow Nova—she must have been doing sixty in a slow-speed zone. So I'm lucky to be alive and here you are demanding your dough right now. Well, I don't have it now, but since she does have insurance and I wasn't at fault in the accident, I'm bound to get paid for the damages. By the way, the repairs on my car are estimated at $450, which is $150 above its market value even though it's in cherry condition—a 1964 Impala with a 283 engine, as you may recall. Believe me, unless I hear from her company within the month I'm going straight to my lawyer.

I applied for a loan, but my father has to co-sign for me, and he won't be back from his Great Books seminar for another ten days.

I can't pay you back because that jerk *I* loaned money to hasn't paid *me*.

How can I return your twenty when you already owe me thirty?

Will you accept merchandise instead? I have five cartons of Dixie cups in my garage.

Let's toss for the whole pot.

I'm filing for bankruptcy.

Other strategies guaranteed to buy you extra time:

Send a check but forget to sign it.

Make out a check for the correct amount but put a different creditor's name on the "Pay To" line.

Enter two different figures on the check: $8.00 on the first line, One Hundred and Forty and 12/100 on the second.

Why I'm a Cheapskate

I can get the same item at K-Mart for half the price.

My uncle can get it for me at wholesale.

Name brands are for suckers. I happen to know that this scotch I buy at Thrifty Drug for $3.99 is really Cutty Sark under a different label.

You may laugh because this wine costs only two bucks a gallon, but it won five gold medals in a blind taste test in Bordeaux, France.

Actually we find that the ground turkey makes better-tasting spaghetti sauce than ground beef—and there's much less fat on it.

We prefer the wings. They are the most flavorful part.

I'll have to opt for the hamburger steak on account of my dentures.

The reason I'm asking you to bring your own mix and snacks is to encourage everyone to do the same thing in the future. That way we can all get together a lot more often without the burden of a big overhead.

Most of the fancy restaurants in this town are ripoffs. They sock you for a lot of phony atmosphere and feed you gunk. You have to know the little out-of-the-way spots if you want the best chow—like the fantastic beef stew at Max's Lunchroom, my greatest discovery. By the way, that's where I'm taking you tonight.

Good furniture doesn't age, it appreciates. That's why we buy all of ours at the Thrift Store.

I was shopping around for an LTD or Impala when my uncle, a super mechanic, told me how badly these new cars are put together and advised me to go for an antique classic as a much better investment. Luckily I latched onto a rare '65 Dart GT with the oversized slant-six. It's almost cherry—or will be when I replace the torn headliner and find some hubcaps.

Believe it or not, this Timex is more accurate than my dad's Seiko. And mine can be dropped from tall buildings.

We were going to buy the big four-bedroom model with the bonus room, but our accountant advised us that the best investment is the least expensive model in a new tract. Besides, we can always add on a kitchen when we really need it.

We don't believe in buying a lot of costly electrical toys that will only be broken the first time they're used.

Why spend a bundle on kids' clothes when they outgrow them in a month?

Why spoil them?

Why pay to see a movie when you can catch one just as good on TV?

You can keep your Paris and London. We're still seeing America first.

Walking will be good for us.

It's the thought that counts.

Why I Spent Too Much

You only live once.

We were going to buy the small bungalow, but our realtor advised us that the best investment is the big two-story model since it contains more construction material and the rise in the cost of the material is the real source of the appreciation.

Comparing a cheap ten-speed bike with a slightly more expensive one is like comparing night and day. With one you bust your gut, but with the other you take that uphill stretch like a breeze. And after all, $150 isn't much when you consider that a professional will spend over a thousand for the model with the graphite frame.

When you've worked as long and hard as I have, you deserve to drive a Cadillac.

When you buy a used car, you're only buying someone else's troubles.

The last guy who dated her always took her to Las Vegas for the weekend in his own Lear jet. I couldn't come on like a miser.

Nothing's too good for my sweetheart.

I had to make up for all the extravagant things they've done for me.

Christmas only comes once a year.

I felt sorry for the salesman.

To the casual eye there is not much difference between a suit by Robert Hall and one by Givenchy, but my clients are catty snobs and I have to be very careful about my image.

I've never had a really decent pair of shoes in my life before.

Quiana shirts are the only kind that don't give me a rash.

There is no wine worth drinking that costs less than ten dollars.

I realize these organic foods cost more, but how can you put a price tag on your family's health?

Nobody tipped me off that that restaurant caters to movie stars and types like Kissinger. It's a good thing I had my Bank-Americard.

I misread the price tag.

I thought he was picking up the tab.

What the hell, I won the money in a poker game.

I always blow off a small percentage of my paycheck. It's good for the soul.

The auctioneer thought I was bidding when I was only scratching my nose.

He had a rotten life. The least we could do was give him a first-class send-off.

I was terribly spoiled as a child.

They may charge more, but they service what they sell.

With some things it doesn't pay to get a bargain.

Besides, it's tax-deductible.

Why I've Never Saved a Dime

My business advisor ripped me off.

I had a timid tax accountant.

I never got around to taking Economics.

All my savings went into Rhodesian real estate.

I joined the Baptists.

Being good Catholics, we have seven kids and twins on the way.

My son decided to study medicine at Harvard. All that our college savings fund covered was his textbooks for the first quarter and two rolls of uppers.

I owed it to my mother to set her up in that luxury retirement villa.

My wife hates to cook, so we dine in restaurants.

My husband still thinks it's cheaper to rent.

My daughter married an actor.

My brother is a bookie.

My parents convinced me that it was classier to be a loan officer in a bank than a plumber.

I got a bargain on a used Ferrari needing "minor engine work."

I ran an independent gas station.

I'm in my third year of analysis.

All my spare change goes into the maintenance of those three slum houses I inherited.

I could never resist a good sales pitch.

You have to have money to make money.

I became a true Christian and gave it all away.

CHAPTER *12*

Arriving Late

To a Parent

The dance was supposed to end at eleven, but it actually went on to twelve-thirty, and I was having so much fun that I didn't even notice.

She introduced me to her parents, and they liked me so much they invited me to stay for dinner. Sorry about missing out on those Big Macs.

I crashed on their sofa and must have fallen asleep because the next thing I knew it was three in the morning.

He decided he wanted to get married, and I had to convince him that we should wait till we're at least seventeen.

He choked on a piece of beef, and I had to call the paramedics and then ride with him to the hospital.

The reason the movie ended so late was that they threw in a special sneak preview of the new Steve McQueen flick. How could I pass up such a freebie?

The game went to sixteen innings. Boy, am I pooped!

The drama coach thought the dress rehearsal stank and made us do it all over again.

My car ran out of gas.

His car only runs in second gear.

My ride home vanished, so I spent an hour waiting at a bus stop before somebody told me the busses don't run after eleven. I ended up hitchhiking half the way and walking the rest.

A dirty old man started chasing me. I had to hide in a frozen-food locker for an hour.

But I *told* you it was going to be a slumber party.

My watch stopped.

To a Spouse

The phone was busy when I called to tell you I'd be late.

The instructor kept our class going an extra hour tonight.

The boss thought we could beat our deadline if we pitched in till eleven.

I ran into a very dear old friend. Of the same sex, naturally.

I know I'm late and smell of perfume. You see, one of my co-workers and his girl friend got drunk at the office party and I had to drive them home. Naturally she sat between us in the front seat, and she always reeks of that stuff. (Wince with disgust at the imposition and refuse to say more about it.)

That guy whose wife just left him started talking about killing himself. I took him out for a drink and tried to calm him down.

The elevator broke down. I was stuck on the tenth floor for thirty-five minutes.

I was headed for the 22nd floor and the elevator bypassed it. I finally got out at the 25th and decided to walk the three flights back down. The only trouble was that the stairwell doors had one-way locks. I couldn't get out even though I banged on that door for ten minutes. I ended up having to walk down all 22 flights, and I'd still be stuck in there if a security guard hadn't heard me screaming and kicking.

There was a bomb scare in the parking lot. The cops held us back for two hours.

But it's a brand-new car! I can't drive it faster than thirty until it passes the thousand mark.

I was trying to run down a jacket I thought would look great on you, but the sale was all over.

I'll be honest. Knowing how much you despise them, I went to a porno movie alone.

I was about to beg off, and then I drew four aces.

The Missed Connection

I was there. Where the hell were *you*?

You waited for me at Montgomery Ward? But you distinctly said, "Meet me at Sears." And that's where I've been for the past hour, trying on work shoes and looking at new televisions.

Believe me, you said four o'clock, not three! Actually I was there at around three, but thinking I was an hour early I went across the street to McDonald's and waited it out munching on onion rings and reading the *National Enquirer*.

You said you'd be at 301 Elm. Fine. But what happened was that I missed the Third Avenue turnoff, and when I got off at the next one I was in another town and didn't know it because it was too dark to read the signs. I stopped at a gas station and checked a map, and sure enough there was an Elm Street—the wrong one, of course, going north instead of west. Well, I followed it all the way up to 301, and since nobody was there to answer the doorbell I turned around and drove back home.

Somebody told me we had just gone on daylight savings time, so I set my watch back an hour.

Sorry I'm two days late. Only this morning did I realize that I've been using last year's calendar.

Oversleeping

Last night I went to a rock concert, and this morning I couldn't hear the radio alarm. Huh?—speak louder!

The dog pulled out the clock plug.

My mother always wakes me up, and this morning she overslept.

I'm a heavy sleeper, so a month ago I hired an answering service to buzz me every morning. It costs ten bucks a month, but I figure it's worth it if it gets me to work on time. The only problem is that their switchboard broke down this morning and I slept till noon.

I've been suffering from acute insomnia. I try counting sheep and thinking about nothing and I take enough Sominex and bourbon to get crocked, but nothing helps. The damned thing is, I always do fall asleep at around five A.M., and so heavily that I don't hear the alarm, which is precisely what happened this morning. I guess I'll have to ask my doctor for some Seconals, though I hate to go the drug route.

The thermostat on my waterbed went out, and I woke up shivering at one A.M. and never could get back to sleep. I think I've caught a cold besides.

My electric blanket keeps overheating, which gives me those bad dreams that prevent me from getting a real rest.

My wife's uncle is visiting us. He is an insomniac who has to watch the *Late Show* till three A.M. Just when I'm about to doze off, I catch a tune from "Top Hat" or "Swing Time" and I'm wide awake tapping my feet against the bedframe.

The walls of our apartment are so tissue-paper thin that we

pick up all the lurid details of our neighbors' nocturnal combat.

The man across the street is building his own catamaran. His radial saw shrieks away night after night.

Some kids on trail bikes were putt-putting in the fields behind our house until dawn. I called the cops and they promised to send a unit over, but evidently they forgot.

CHAPTER *13*

Dodging Chores

You must be kidding. Do yard work on Easter Sunday? (Or Christmas, Thanksgiving, Lincoln's Birthday, Arbor Day, Flag Day, etc.)

It's too sunny to clean the pool. The glare makes it hard to see what you're doing. And we're out of chemicals.

There's no point in fixing that door today. It's so damp that the wood is probably shrunken half an inch all around. It would be impossible to take accurate measurements.

I've been advised that cement work should only be done by professionals.

Wash the car without a chamois on a hot day like this? It'll be so blotched and speckled it will look worse than dirty.

How can I do the dishes when there is no hot water?

Do you think I want to go to school with dishpan hands?

I'm too clumsy. Whenever I wash them I break half of them.

How can I mow the lawn when it's so wet? And look at the rocks and doggy poop all over the place. Besides, the mower is out of gas and somebody filled the gas can with ethyl instead of regular. Naturally the service stations are all closed, today being Sunday.

The last time I cut the grass my hay fever flared up so badly I was wiped out for the whole weekend, a sopping, whimpering mess. It will have to wait till I get the results of my allergy check and some decent vaccine.

I'm in pain with inflammed epididymites, which are those cords that go into and out of the testicles. Heavy lifting is a no-no.

You know how I hurt my back last year? Well, I must have slept on it the wrong way because it's killing me all over again.

Before fertilizing the lawn, let's wait till rain is predicted. We have to consider the water shortage.

Before fixing the roof, we had better wait for rain to find out where it leaks.

I loaned our pruner to the next door neighbors, and they're gone for the weekend.

I have a feeling that the elm is only playing dead. Let's wait a little longer before cutting it down.

I'll be happy to transform that tree into firewood if I can borrow somebody's chain saw. It would take a week to do it by hand.

I can't vacuum the carpet because I just washed my hair.

I can't take the trash out because I just put on my best suit.

I can't babysit because I have a bad cold and don't want the tot to catch it.

I'll try to get on it later today, but first I have to work on my car (or outboard motor, stereo, electric typewriter, etc.).

Let's let it get a little dirtier. That way we'll save on the detergent.

I didn't get the ironing done because Mary needed my advice on what to buy for her sister's wedding. We must've hit five department stores before she finally made up her mind.

Sorry, but I'm due on the golf course in fifteen minutes, and I doubt if I'll have enough leftover energy when I get back.

You are supposed to help your sisters wash the dishes. As soon as the customary after-dinner conversation begins, you silently slip into the living room and commence practicing the piano. When it is time to clear the table, you are totally ensnared in a Chopin mazurka. The other girls are furious, but your mother tells them, "Leave her alone. I only wish the two of you could be so inspired."

CHORES AS AN EXCUSE: Reverse the excuses in the preceding section. Also see Chapter 4, "The House."

CHAPTER *14*

Dodging Meetings

⮜ A good general ploy is to join two or three other committees. Not only will you gain a reputation as a commendably public-spirited individual, but you will always be able to say, "Sorry I got my wires crossed. Tonight's the night I make my quarterly report to the Security Committee." Also, "Gee, I guess I'm spreading myself too thin."

I wasn't notified in time.

I didn't think you'd hold a meeting on Lincoln's Birthday.

Nobody told me you had changed the meeting place.

I came last week when the meeting was canceled. I didn't know you'd rescheduled it for tonight.

I didn't think I was still a member since I never got a receipt for my payment of dues.

I thought you were only holding elections, and I sent you my proxy vote.

I thought it was an ad hoc committee and that we'd already hocked.

I can't be on that subcommittee when I'm on this subcommittee.

None of those meetings are legal until we appoint a secretary who can take the minutes properly.

That last session was utterly chaotic. I refuse to come back until we get a parliamentarian who knows how to read *Robert's Rules of Order.*

Since it's an anti-pollution organization, I thought we would be dealing with smog, but all they ever talk about is noise pollution.

Being an avid trail-biker myself, I feel there is a conflict of interest here somewhere.

It seems like I'm doing all the work around here.

Too much "groupthink" is bogging us down. I think I could do a better job if I tackled it alone.

Let's take a moratorium for a month and honestly ask ourselves, "What are we really accomplishing?"

CHAPTER 15

Dodging Invitations

The Spur-of-the-Moment Summons

We're in the middle of painting the living room. I know it's awfully late, but this is the only time we don't have the dog and the kids under our feet.

I know it's early, but I just took a warm bath and a Seconal and I'm practically in slumberland.

I've made enough dough for six loaves of bread, and I was just popping the first one into the oven when you called.

We couldn't miss the final chapter of ABC's novel for television.

My boss called to ask me over for a drink. He's having marital problems and seems desperately in need of someone to confide in.

We were just on our way out the front door. We're spending the day at a friend's mountain cabin and may stay over for the weekend.

My husband is working overtime and I never go anywhere without him.

Sorry, but it's taken me a month to square things with my wife for my beastly behavior at that last drunken bash you threw on the spur of the moment.

Tomorrow is my early day at work. I'd hate to drop in and then have to rush right back out again.

A ring of burglars has been working our block, and I still haven't wired up my new alarm system.

We all have strep throat.

Our car would never make it that far.

We would never find a baby sitter this late.

(Also see Chapter 22, "Breaking Off Phone Conversations," and review the Catch-Alls.)

The Advance-Notice Summons

Gee, we're spending that weekend at a state park campground. We had to make those reservations three months in advance.

If I'm lucky I'll be flying to London for a sales convention right about then.

I'm afraid our season ticket for the opera will tie us up for six Saturdays in a row.

I'm working with a suicide-prevention center, and I have to be on call seven nights a week.

Sorry, but that's the night of my kid's graduation (or confirmation, school play, piano recital, Pop Warner game, Little League game, etc.).

My wife will be out of town that week, and she would be sore if I went without her.

Grandmother will be visiting us.

Since I've discovered that I have an addictive reaction (or ulcer, diabetes, prostate infection), I can't risk even the tiniest sip of any alcoholic beverage. I'm afraid the temptation would be too great if I came to one of your lively parties.

That's the evening of the day I go to my endodonist for a retro-fill, which involves cutting the gum down below the roots and leaves you with a melon-sized jaw for days afterwards. I'm damn sure I won't be up to any socializing.

That's around the time I'm scheduled to have some fatty tissue removed from my eyelids, and they tell me the bruises always take weeks to go away. That's blepharoplasty for you.

I might be able to come and then again I might not. It all depends on my father's condition after his open-heart surgery.

Hope I can make it. It all depends on whether or not my lawyer can swing a postponement of my arraignment.

I'm taking my vacation early this year.

Sacred Family Gatherings

Dad, I have to work on Thanksgiving. Since Thursday's my normal day off, my holiday fell on Monday. The problem is that one of the other guys is taking his week's vacation and I have to sub for him. Do you follow me?

We won a free turkey dinner for two at the best restaurant in town. It comes with drinks and a top-notch show, and frankly it's the first thing we've ever won in our lives. We figured you'd understand. Listen, if we get through early we'll drop by to say hello to you and the family. But don't count on it.

(*To Mom*) I can't make it for Christmas because we have to go over to John's mother's. She's sick and I'm helping her with the cooking.

(*To John's Mom*) We're going over to my mom's for dinner. She's sick and I'm helping her with the cooking—and John's going to help my dad fix his car for work tomorrow. (*Then you stay home and spend Christmas alone together.*)

I'm sorry I missed Aunt Joan's funeral. The truth is, I had nothing to wear but my maroon blazer and I don't even own a necktie. I went to a tux shop to see if I could rent a dark suit, but all they had was party-type outfits with ruffled shirts. I heard about another place, but it was closed when I got there. May she rest in peace.

Don't tell anyone, but the reason I missed Sue's birthday was that my paycheck got held up and I was ashamed to come without that Mickey Mouse watch I've been promising her for six months. I'll mail it next Friday.

> *Dear Mom,*
> *I regret that I won't be able to see you on Sunday, Mother's Day, but after pondering this customary event I have come to some sad conclusions. First, what started out as a warm and intimate family celebration has deteriorated into a gigantic ripoff of the American consumer, a big-business scheme to pressure us into buying second-rate merchandise which isn't needed anyway as a token of our love for Mom. Second, I resent anyone's designating a certain day for praising Mom. What about the rest of the year?*
> *—Your Loving Son.*

Tupperware Parties, Crystal Parties, Lingerie Parties, Wine-Tasting Parties, Macramé Parties, Fashion Jewelry Parties, Baby Showers, and Political Coffees

My uncle is head buyer for Federated Restaurant Supplies, and he has given us so much Tupperware stuff that we can't find room to store it.

Oddly enough, I've promised to go to a Revere Ware party the same night you're throwing your Tupperware party.

My great aunt collected crystal pieces for over forty years. She died last month and I was her sole beneficiary.

In our house that kind of stuff is only good for collecting dust.

If I wear any of those slinky nylon or rayon things I break out in a ghastly rash. My doctor has ordered nothing but cotton, but usually I wear nothing at all.

I let my husband buy all my lingerie according to his own kinky tastes.

Count me out of the wine party. I burned my tongue on a baked potato.

I hate the taste of wine, and it gives me a headache.

You say they're pushing California reds? Ugh! Show me a good Rhône or Bordeaux and I go into ecstasies, but Napa Valley is for the birds.

My daughter is learning to do macramé at high school, and I've promised to buy all her stuff at the next art sale, which is on Sunday.

My beauty counselor forbids me, with my build and coloring, to wear any jewelry except a couple of simple cultured-pearl pieces, and my husband is buying me those for our anniversary.

I swore off all baby showers when only three people showed up for mine.

Your candidate sounds like a live one, but I've just switched my party affiliation. Someday when you have three hours to spare, I'll try to tell you why and see if I can't win you over to my way of thinking.

I swore off all politics after Watergate.

Until my husband gets his cost-of-living increase, he has vetoed all excess spending.

Leaving Early

(1) Since goodbyes can take an hour, especially when all your friends are half pickled, a good tactic is to sneak away quietly when nobody is looking. To smoothe things over, send your host a thank-you note the next day.

(2) Have a pre-planned exit visa: the late airport pickup, the other gathering you have to drop in on, the baby-sitter who must

be in by eleven. To pave the way, cast a few concerned glances at your wristwatch, murmur audibly to your spouse, and ask your host for a little coffee.

(3) Have your sitter phone you about some problem with the kids or pets that demands your immediate attention.

(4) Start acting drunk. Make a pass at the hostess, fall down, and ask for a *lot* of coffee.

CHAPTER *16*

Withholding Invitations

To Would-Be Drop-Ins

We're leaving on our vacation and hope to make it to Cleveland by midnight. We'll send you a postcard.

The bathroom pipes just exploded. There's nothing anyone can do except the plumber and he's on his way.

I guess it's all right, though the Balthazers are coming over any second. (*Say it with distaste, knowing they hate the Balthazars.*)

My sister and brother-in-law have been separated for two weeks, and they decided to come over here and have me play marriage counselor. The fur's about to fly, so you'd better stay out of it.

We're all down with dysentery.

We're just starting dinner.

(Again, review the Catch-Alls.)

To Solicitors

My aunt sells Avon goods, too, and I order all of mine through her.

I'm in public relations and my agency pays for all the magazines I need. Right now they're coming out of my ears.

I just bought an air conditioner from your competitor.

I plan to hold off on buying a swimming pool until I'm sure there will be enough water to go around for everyone.

My freezer is still loaded with all those Girl Scout cookies I bought from you kids a year ago.

The last time I ordered a pre-cut side of beef it was sixty percent bones, fat, and gristle.

I'm raising my own steer and plan to slaughter it myself in June.

I'm boycotting all Japanese products until they agree to stop killing off all the whales.

I can't use it, but why don't you talk to those new people down the street?

I'm only leasing this house. Talk to the owner.

I'm about to be laid off.

I have to be careful with my money. Does *Consumer Reports* rate your product as a "best buy"?

First I'd have to check you out with the Better Business Bureau.

Why should I care whether or not your five-hundreth subscription wins you a trip to Daytona Beach when my own son can't even find a summer job?

My kids have read halfway through the *Encyclopedia Brittanica*, so who needs your dummy *World Book*?

CHAPTER *17*

To the Traffic Cop

◄§ Most of your attempts to sway the patrolman will flop for the simple reason that his decision on whether or not to cite you has been made irrevocably during the moments before his actual approach to your vehicle. For the dreamer in you, here are the standard tactics.

I just gunned it for a second to make a safe lane change.

I thought you were after someone else, so I sped up to get out of your way.

I had the rock station on so loud I couldn't hear your siren.

That Porsche up ahead was going faster than I and weaving like crazy? Why didn't you pull him over?

Yes, it's possible that the light was red, but it was yellow when I reached the intersection, and then I saw that the guy behind me just wasn't about to stop, so by darting forward I prevented an accident from happening.

I was coming down the hill and didn't notice that I'd gained speed.

Gee, Officer, I didn't realize that I was going so fast, but I'm glad you stopped me because I might have caused an accident. You see, I've just spent the whole day in court getting divorced, and I'm pretty upset with the results. (The cop may sympathize as he bitterly resents all the unpaid time he must spend in court himself. Also, according to an occupational survey, policemen have the highest rate of divorce.)

My old lady just put three-hundred dollars onto my American Express card and we had a helluva fight and she threw me out. So give me your ticket. That'll clinch a perfect day.

I guess I *was* in a hurry, Officer. My father, whom I haven't laid eyes on for a year, just got moved from San Quentin to the honor farm. I wangled a permit to see him just for today, and visiting time ends at four.

I was on my way to see my little girl in the hospital.

I'm ten minutes late for a job interview.

I was just driving home from college. I'm a police science major and I work part-time for Burns Security Agency. I used to be a Deputy Explorer at the sheriff's station. How about it?

I just spent $400 for an engine overhaul, and I was just giving it a brief shakedown test in the empty lane.

I had to go through that stop sign because something is wrong with my engine. Every time I stop she dies and won't start up again. (You had better hope that happens when the man asks for a demonstration.)

I heard my motor mount break loose; if I'd stopped suddenly I might have caused a nasty accident.

My throttle was stuck.

My speedometer gets stuck at fifty-five and just stays there.

But Officer, my car can't go that fast.

That huge moving van obstructed my view of the sign.

I thought the Automobile Club was going to take care of that ticket for me. I'll be sure to remind them.

Sir, I picked up a hitchhiker and he pulled out this funny-looking little cigarette and began smoking it, and those are his leavings that you hold in your hand, Sir. Next time I'll be more wary.

(He stops you for speeding. As usual he asks, "Do you know why I pulled you over?") Yes, my right rear light doesn't work and you wanted to tell me about it. Now please don't let me go without a citation or my husband will never bother to fix it. (Hopefully you are cited only for the defective light.)

Officer, I always ride my bike close to the white line. It's the softest place and the middle of the lane is too oily.

The only reason I crossed over the line is because this idiot behind me keeps shifting her weight to get comfortable.

(For some authentic and quite crazy traffic accident summaries, see page 185.)

CHAPTER *18*

To the Teacher

I left that paper in my mom's car and forgot to take it out before she drove off to work this morning.

I got halfway through the final draft and my typewriter broke down. It was midnight, too late to borrow another one. I hesitate to hand in a sloppy-looking pencil draft. Can I be excused till Monday on this one?

My three-year-old niece used my term paper to color on, and my mother threw it away thinking it was scrap paper.

I was absent the day you assigned it.

I thought it was due *next* Friday.

I've been preparing for the exam all week, and last night I got off to work at two A.M. and slept right through the alarm. Can't you let me take a makeup?

I can't afford to buy the textbook until my Veteran's check comes in.

Somebody ripped off my text and I had to ask a friend to loan me his. Well, he didn't remember to bring it over until last night, and that's why I only got through half of the assigned chapter. I mean, that's a long chapter.

My text is used, and would you believe that the college book-store goofed and sold me an earlier edition with different page numbers? I guess I read all the wrong selections.

I enrolled in this class late and didn't catch the first two lectures.

I thought it was going to be an essay test, so I concentrated on basic concepts rather than specific facts.

I have memory lapses, but I'm making great progress with the school psychologist.

I'm dyslexic, but I'm working on it by taking classes in spelling and reading fundamentals.

I didn't feel ready for that test because, frankly, a couple of the main concepts involved are still too confusing. You offered to give us outside help, and though I've tried three times to catch you in your office you never seem to be available.

I'm visually oriented, and you haven't shown enough movies.

I thought this was a remedial class. You're going too fast for me.

I thought this was going to be an advanced class. I can't get back to fundamentals.

I've been going downhill ever since we started those group sessions. All the other kids ever discuss is their cars and sex.

You haven't motivated me.

I don't think your approach is relevant to what is happening in the world today.

My job takes up too much of my time, though I'm trying.

I'm in the middle of a marital breakup.

I got sick on those hamburgers they serve in the school cafeteria.

Just as I was driving into the college parking lot, some joker ran up and told me that school had been closed down because of a bomb threat.

Please let me add this class! It's the only one that fits into my schedule because of my work hours, and if I don't make it I won't have enough credits to graduate and I'll have to go to summer school. That also means I'll miss out on a European vacation that my parents have been planning for me all year.

I can't graduate unless you change that C to a B.

CHAPTER **19**

To the Coach and Spectator

◆§ Excuses for blowing your game are usually as futile as those to the highway patrolman or the irate spouse, but here goes.

I thought it was an outside pitch.

I wanted to make the pitcher look good for a change.

The field was muddy.

The bat was broken and the merest fraction of an ounce can make all the difference.

I didn't take the three warmup swings, only two, and that threw me. I just didn't feel right—couldn't get psyched up.

Our new coach is from Puerto Rico. He just doesn't understand American-style playing.

I couldn't have cared less after that insulting pep talk.

I was never cut out to be a linebacker.

I should have stuck with basketball.

I wasn't wearing my own socks, and that slowed me down. And when I hit the take-off board a gust of wind knocked me off balance and I fell into the side of the pit.

No wonder I missed. Just look at the feathers on these arrows—they're multilated!

I had to borrow my partner's rifle, and it was improperly sighted.

I could have met that serve if it hadn't been for a drop of perspiration in my eye. Next time I'll bring my sweat-band.

I wasn't concentrating.

The sun got in my eyes.

I'm out of practice. I'll just have to start playing more.

I guess I'm getting too old for these strenuous games.

Winning is a childish aim. I play for the fun of it.

CHAPTER *20*

Religion Found and Lost

Why God Comes First

I gave up those wild parties when I mad my decision for Christ.

We'll have to attend my nephew's confirmation (or baptism, bar mitzvah, ordination, etc.).

I'm late for choir practice.

I'm teaching a Sunday school class.

Sunday school was cancelled, so I don't have anyplace to leave my kids.

Six of the parish kids had no way to get out to the church camp, so I volunteered my microbus.

The vicar is coming by for tea and cookies.

I couldn't afford $40 an hour for therapy, so I thought I would try a little free pastoral counseling. Dr. Jones seems like a good listener, and he is very generous with his port wine.

I'm the bingo croupier at tonight's bazaar.

I've volunteered to mimeograph the weekly worship bulletin.

I've joined a mission to spread the light to Omaha.

I'm planning to marry a Catholic, and I have to go over to the church for an indoctrination.

The IRS keeps questioning my claim for church donations, so I thought I would go over there and drop a few bills into the collection plate.

Sorry, but my religion forbids the consumption of alcoholic beverages (or coffee, tea, Pepsi-cola, meat, eggs, pasta, etc.).

Church is the only place I can afford to take my girlfriend.

Did you get a look at our new female minister? Wow!

I found it.

Why I Didn't Go to Services

I can't attend Communion because I haven't been to confession.

Last Sunday, when the minister told off the whole congregation, he kept looking at me in particular. I was too embarrassed to go back.

Frankly, I was broke that weekend and ashamed to attend with only a nickle for the collection plate.

The sanctuary is always too chilly, and I was coming down with a cold.

They ought to turn on their air conditioner in the middle of July.

I have back trouble. Sitting in one of those wooden pews would only aggravate it.

How can I genuflect with this messed-up knee?

Since my body is the temple, I just stayed home by myself.

Why I've Dropped Out

Churches distract me. I only feel close to God when I'm standing by the ocean or walking through the piney woods.

I've stopped going ever since I realized that the Bible is a bundle of contradictions and the priesthood a gang of money-grubbing hypocrites.

They want too many donations, and I've heard it all goes to support their administrative bureaucracy.

Their doctrine has no relevance to what is happening in the world.

I can't stomach the way these new young liberal preachers try to make everything "relevant." I'll look at my newspaper when I need a political editorial.

Haven't you heard that they are putting in female ministers? That's too far out for me.

I've decided to switch over to Episcopalian. I prefer their ritual.

The acoustics in that church were so bad I could never hear the sermon.

I couldn't stand the rowdy congregation. You meet a better class of people in a kennel.

The preacher always puts me to sleep.

He made too many references to sex.

If God exists, then why are there wars, social injustices, and starving babies?

I lost it.

CHAPTER **21**

The Unsent Letter, Card Or Gift

◆§ Never say "The letter I wrote you must have been lost in the mails." Instances of postage truly lost are still too rare to be believable. Since most letters are written in answer to other letters, a smarter approach is to take the offensive: "I think it was you who owed me the last letter. Did you write me? The reason I ask is that a couple of kids on our block recently got caught for raiding mailboxes. Lately I've been getting lots of follow-ups on bills I never received in the first place, so I figure I must've been one of their targets. What's that? You say you did write me last month? Ah, that explains it."

> *Dear Bill,*
>
> *My only excuse for not having written before is my new job. Hardly a week goes by that I'm not called in on special overtime to ward off some new crisis. Weekends too. Really, I seem to have no time left even for the wife and kids. If this keeps on I'm going to quit. Life is too short.*

> *Dear Maureen,*
>
> *My agent finally got me a deal with Random House. There is a July deadline for the prospectus, which means I'm rewriting around the clock, or until*

I collapse from exhaustion. On my off hours I have to play tennis or drive long distances just to get my eyes back in shape. Needless to say, I'm behind on all my letters.

Dear Louise,
Believe it or not, I wrote you a fifteen-page letter explaining my true feelings, and when I read it over it sounded so pretentious I had to destroy it. So here, in the simplest possible language, is the way I think things really stand between us. . . .

Dear George,
What I have to tell you is too complicated and personal to put into writing. Let's meet for lunch when you get back into town.

You're such a terrific letter writer that I feel utterly inadequate whenever I sit down to answer you. If only I could plug my brain into some Shakespeare's.

I smashed my writing hand in the refrigerator door.

My IBM typewriter broke down and I can't think through a ballpoint pen. Also my handwriting is atrocious.

I dictate all my letters, and my secretary is still on her leave of absence.

I know you gave me your new address, but I couldn't remember where I'd jotted it down. I searched the house for it twice over, and only today did it finally turn up—on the back of my water bill!

I ran out of my special monogrammed stationery right in the middle of the letter, and I'm still waiting for the reorder.

Frankly, I'm afraid to use the mails after reading that article about the gross inefficiency of the Postal Service.

I've decided to boycott them after that last outrageous rate increase.

My four-year-old son begged me to let him take your letter down to the mailbox. Did it ever arrive?

Grandma, I've only learned the aphabet up to the letter V.

This year I sent no Christmas card to you or anybody else since the whole thing seems to have turned into a big commercial hustle.

I sent Buddy down to the drug store to buy a card for you, and the one he picked was so dreadful I couldn't bring myself to send it. The next day I went there myself, and the ones I saw were even cornier—all gaudy pink flowers and sickeningly sentimental verses. I made up my mind to go to a good stationery store, but I just never got around to it.

December was so sunny out here in California that we forgot all about Christmas.

The store's wrapping department promised to deliver that gift. I'll have to call them and find out what happened to it.

My surprise homemade present still isn't quite finished. Look for it in about six weeks.

I was hoping we might agree to stop sending each other presents on account of the inflationary prices.

> *Dear Diane,*
> *I conscientiously made a record of all my friends'*
> *birthdays and somehow I got yours mixed up with*
> *Sid's. By now he ought to be halfway through that*
> *bottle of Lady Clairol I meant for you.*

CHAPTER **22**

Breaking Off Phone Conversations

⌐§ Shun timeworn dodges like "Something's cooking on the stove," "Someone's at the door," and "This call must be costing you a fortune, so I'll let you go." If nothing better strikes you, simply break the connection in the middle of a sentence, place a weighty object on the receiver bar, and wait a long time before hanging up. The next time you see your caller, explain how hard you tried to get back in touch—but evidently the phone was out of order.

We've been watching our neighbor's little boy, and suddenly he's very sick. I called his doctor's answering service for advice and they're going to call us right back, so I've got to keep this line clear.

Oh-oh, here comes that gossip from up the street—you know, the one who hangs around all afternoon guzzling my jug wine. Listen, do me a favor. About three minutes from now call me back and we'll act like you've got some emergency and keep talking until she leaves. (*When the phone rings three minutes later, don't answer it.*)

My God, a policeman is running across my front lawn waving his revolver!

My car is rolling down the driveway into the street. Catch you later.

Say, I've got to run to the john fast.

The main pipe in the wall just burst open, and I'm standing in water. Christ, I could get electrocuted! (*Hang up fast.*)

Wait, I hear the cat crying! Do you know she's been missing for the past five days?

Listen, I was supposed to pick Anna up at her dance class five minutes ago.

I heard a click and I think I'm being tapped.

Or was it only those snoops on my party line? I'll call you back from a booth.

I'm in a booth and I just plunked in my last quarter, so make it fast.

Do you know that it costs me more to call you thirty miles away than it costs to call my brother in New York after six P.M.

I can't answer such a technical question right off the top of my head. Give me an hour to go through my files and records and then call me back.

Mom and Dad limited me to a half hour. So finish what you've got to say in the next forty-five seconds.

Your voice sounds awful. Hang up and call a doctor.

Yours is the most interesting obscene phone call I've had in three weeks, but if I don't take my cookies right out of the oven, they'll be burned and my children will be very upset.

I've got to keep the line open for President Carter's answer to my question about the liquor retailers' pricing agreements.

Pretend to be an answer-phone by announcing in a very formal tone, "Hello there! Although I am not presently at home, I will be happy to take your call and get back to you at a later time. Please state your message at the sound of the chime. . . ."

CHAPTER *23*

Personal Shortcomings

Why I'm Such a Mess

. I never dress up unless I'm going out on a date.

After wearing white shirts and ties at the bank, I just have to let it it all hang out on Saturdays.

Most of my clients are in the counterculture. I've got to play the role.

I'm doing a bit part in a TV pilot about Appalachian coal miners in the thirties.

I work undercover.

Mom, didn't you know that shredded, grubby workshirts are now the "in" look at the most sophisticated cocktail parties?

These pants are tie-dyed, not dirty.

Burglars cleaned out my wardrobe. I was lucky I had these overalls stashed away in the attic.

I was helping a friend clean out his garage, and I didn't have time to go home and change.

I came over without bathing because I planned to take a dip in your pool.

The main water line broke, so there went my weekly shower.

I can't bear to sit in dirty water.

After seeing "Jaws," I can't bear to set foot in any water.

I hate bathing alone, and my girlfriend is out of town this weekend.

My doctor forbids me to shave or scrub until my rash clears up.

Mud baths have been prescribed for my condition.

I ran out of stick deodorant.

My cold kept me from detecting my own offensive odor.

My discount barber decided that he was a hair stylist.

My hairdresser used acid instead of alkaline.

My girl gets her kicks from dirty, ornery-looking men.

D. H. Lawrence once wrote that a little dirt is good for the blood.

After forty-three years of gussying up, I think I've earned the right to just be myself.

What you see is what you get!

Why I Seemed Rude

I'm just shy with new people.

Whenever I'm nice to people they always take advantage of me.

I wasn't grim. I was looking for the toilet.

I got an unaccountable erection and was trying to grimace it down.

It's just my time of the month.

I couldn't smile on account of my split lip.

Did I ever claim to be Mr. Nice Guy?

I couldn't greet your mother because she was talking to you and I never interrupt.

I didn't realize he was your minister. He sounded more like a subscription salesman for *Hustler*.

He had bad teeth and shifty eyes.

She didn't say hello to you.

He kept staring up your skirt.

A cocktail kiss isn't supposed to include two inches of tongue.

He said the Lakers would cream the Hawks.

She made a bitchy remark about Amy's nanny.

She kept pointing at me and giggling like I was Groucho Marx.

He still owes me a hundred bucks.

I think that shrimpy intellectual was insulting me with those words "sedulous" and "empathetic."

I don't enjoy being labeled a male chauvinist pig—especially by some dumb broad.

I've learned the hard way that it doesn't pay to be nice to that person. Give her and inch and she'll take a mile.

I couldn't risk getting cornered by that bore for the whole evening.

I caught her saying "Yecch" at the escargot in my salad.

But you'll just never understand our love-hate relationship.

I'll be nice to them when you start being nice to my buddies down at the snooker parlor.

That's just our kind of wacko humor with each other.

I was only doing my face-stretching exercise.

But you always tell me I'm beautiful when I'm angry.

It's taken me five years in group therapy to achieve the ability to tell people what I really think of them.

Why I Got Drunk and Made an Ass of Myself

I'm a scotch-on-the-rocks man, only they ran out of scotch too early, so I switched to bourbon and ginger ale. The sweet stuff does it to me every time.

Those margaritas always taste like soda pop until the curtain falls.

I was under the impression that we were being invited over for dinner as well as cocktails, but all I saw was Fritos and dip. I can never make it on an empty stomach.

This was my first bout with the sauce in months, and my resistance has dwindled to zero. Honest, I only had two.

I knew it was time to leave, and suddenly he announced his daughter's engagement and produced a magnum of champagne.

He got generous and brought out that dusty bottle of thirty-year-old cognac.

The guy is obsessed with keeping your glass filled to the brim. Every time you turn your head he zings in on you, aiming that fifth like a six-gun.

I didn't kiss her—she kissed me!

When I got out of the Marines ten years ago, I swore I would get that s.o.b. if I ever saw him again.

I punched him in the mouth because he made an insulting remark about you.

It was one of those free-for-alls. I was making a mad dash for the exit when some creep's fist landed on my ear.

It wasn't the alcohol, it was the canapés. You should have told me they had chocolate in them because that's my number one allergy irritant. Still, I'm surprised I took swings at all those guests. Usually I only scream and beat my head against the wall.

The owner of the bar said it was his tenth anniversary and insisted on refilling our martini pitcher three times.

Hell, it was New Year's Eve! (Or Christmas, Easter, Valentine's Day, your birthday, your payday, etc.)

Why I'm Still Drinking

A recent study proved that people who drink live longer than people who don't. (Practically anything has been proved by a recent study.)

It's only cheap rotgut that hurts you. I buy nothing but the best bonded stuff.

I have a very high tolerance. I can slosh it down all night and never even get a hangover. So what's the problem?

It's one of the necessities of my business. No martinis for lunch, no sale.

I'm cuter and sexier when I've had a few.

I only do it to keep my husband company.

I wouldn't have any friends left if I went on the wagon.

People would think I was unsophisticated.

You're not a man if you don't know how to hold your liquor.

What would Christmas be without a little eggnog?

A dinner without wine is like a bald-headed woman.

It's a tonic for the blood.

My doctor assures me that a couple of highballs in the evening are good for my digestion.

I need it to unwind after a hectic day at the plant.

Winston Churchill drank a quart of brandy every day.

They called Jesus a wine-bibber, and he was my kind of guy.

If God had wanted man to abstain, he wouldn't have created fermentation.

We're supposed to conserve our water.

I could never stand the taste of iced tea.

What I drink now is nothing compared to what I used to drink.

I know my own limits.

A knowledge of fine wines is the best insurance against old age. When you've lost your ability to see, hear, or walk onto the shuffle-board court, you'll still have your cultivated palate.

I'm crazy about whisky labels and I'm saving them to paper my living room wall.

A subtler evasion is the use of cutesy euphemisms. Instead of requesting a whisky, a tequila on the rocks, or more booze, try asking for some grog, a toddy, a libation, a small martini or one more all around.

Why I'm Still Smoking

I love the taste of good tobacco.

Ever since basic training, when the topkick shouted, "The smoking lamp is lit," I haven't been able to live without that hourly reward.

I do it because my wife does it. I don't want to be a spoilsport.

What's sex without that cigarette you share in bed afterwards?

I grew up under the influence of forties movies. Bogart and Bette Davis built their acting styles around the cigarette, and what would Rita Hayworth be in that satin gown without a backlit halo of smoke?

It's impossible to give up any habit you've had for thirty-five years.

If I quit I will immediately put on weight—everybody does—and even ten extra pounds will be more hazardous for my blood pressure and general health than the smoking itself.

I've tried every method of quitting from tapering off to water filters to electric-shock treatments. I guess hypnotism is next.

The only surefire way is the Swedish method, where they give you injections of nicotine to tide you over. Too bad I can't afford the air fare.

They say that smoking is the hardest addiction in the world to kick—tougher than heroin even. So why fight impossible odds?

It's true that I'm still puffing, but notice that this brand has only five milligrams of tars.

I've cut my quota down to one pack daily—unless somebody makes me very nervous.

My mother and father have been smoking for forty years and they're in fine shape. Immunity from cancer is probably in my genes.

I guess I'm the oral type.

The smog will get you sooner.

I've already got emphysema, so it doesn't make a helluva lot of difference.

I don't have much to live for anyway.

Why I'm Still Overweight

I was born with an extra-long colon.

As a child in the ghetto I never got enough to eat. I'm still making up for it.

They say overweight people are victims of their early eating habits, and I was raised in the back of a German restaurant.

Me overweight? You should have seen me a year ago.

The pounds I lost by dieting were offset by the pounds I put on when I gave up smoking.

Whenever I lose it I gain it back and have to lose it all over again. My doctor tells me the yo-yo effect is worse for my heart than the pounds themselves, so I intend to say the way I am.

I'm funnier when I'm fat.

In grandfather's day, fat was beautiful.

My wife thinks it's sexy to be crushed by three hundred pounds.

My wife still believes that the way to a man's heart is through his stomach. She would be destroyed if I ever refused a third helping of her lasagna.

Can I help it if good cooking is my only real pleasure in life?

It just happens that the only kind of food I like is fattening.

It isn't the food so much as the companionship and pleasant atmosphere of a good restaurant that I would miss.

Eating helps me to forget my personal tragedy.

I've had too many problems with the opposite sex. Being fat keeps me out of the whole silly competition.

My doctor took me off my weight pills because he thought I was turning into a junkie.

He prescribed a lot of tennis, and then I broke my Achilles tendon.

I may look like I'm stuffing myself, but I'm really on a very sophisticated new diet.

Besides, I'm exactly where I ought to be with my height and frame.

It all started when they took me off the sports desk and made me their restaurant reviewer.

Somebody stole my calorie counter.

I stopped worrying when they brought out that Pacer with the extra-wide passenger door.

I just bought a new wardrobe. The cost of alterations would be crippling.

I'm not fat, I'm big. Would you believe large? Husky? Robust?

Why My Whole Life Has Been a Failure

I was the first born. My parents made all their mistakes on me.

They alternately spoiled me and overpunished me, and so I grew up nervous and insecure and lacking in self-discipline.

I was the second born. My big brother got all the confidence in that family, not to mention the brand-new clothes.

My father was a devout Christian, and he instilled in me the virtues of brotherly love and submission to God's will. Not a very good background for success in a capitalistic society, is it?

My father and two older brothers all turned into bums and winos. I had nobody worthwhile to emulate. Say pal, can you spare a quarter?

My college vocational counselor steered me into engineering. Years later I discovered that he had goofed and that my real talent was for the law.

Despite my high grade point, I quit college in my second year and went off to sea. I've been paying for the romantic impulse ever since.

I was too keen on chasing skirts to take my studies seriously.

How could I know that my membership in that pinko college club would become a black mark on my employment chances for the next twenty years?

A very minor jail record—I swiped some bruised apples at age fifteen—has kept me out of every job I've ever really wanted.

The economy was tight in those days. Nobody who wasn't rich went to college. You were lucky to get any job you could find.

I might have made it big if I hadn't been forced to marry my girlfriend and take a factory job at eighteen.

It was a bad marriage. My spouse's country background and crude tastes have always held me back in my climb up the social ladder.

After five years of preparing to become a teacher, I discovered I had an allergy to chalk dust.

I lost my one chance at a big promotion when I refused to sleep with the supervisor.

I made too many enemies.

It's not my fault that I was born so handsome that nobody ever took me seriously.

When you've got an ugly face like mine, you can expect to be passed over for all the pretty personality-plus types.

It's hard to succeed in business if you're a Jew (or a black, Mexican, Pole, Italian, Armenian, Texan, Southern Baptist, Catholic, female, homosexual, etc., etc.).

I was always the Good Samaritan—gave too many people goods on the cuff.

To make it big you have to brown-nose your way into supervision, and frankly I've been too happy at my craft to want to do anything else.

I made some sour investments and had to sell out, leave town, and start all over again. I'll be back up there yet.

The mob edged me out of my little business.

I worked so hard for so many years that I finally had a nervous breakdown. Now I'm glad to be out of the rat race.

My career as a prize-winning photographer ended when I developed tunnel vision. So what's wrong with selling used cars?

They detected a rather raucous heart murmur and told me to ease up.

My spirit was broken by a chain of family tragedies.

Booze done it.

The critics loved my work, but the masses didn't pay for it. I was ten years before my time.

My wife spent all our savings on fur coats and jewelry and then ran out on me.

My husband gambled it all away.

My company went bankrupt and I lost all hope of a pension.

I rear-ended a guy in a Ford while my liability insurance was lapsed. Now all my dough goes into that whiplash.

I never had enough time to get it all together.

Work is overrated. I prefer just lying here in the sun.

(Also see "Why I've Never Saved a Dime," page 118.)

CHAPTER 24

Oneupmanship

Why We Can't Go Where You Want to Go

The *Times* says that restaurant recycles it own food.

I hear they put dog food in their burger meat.

We'll go there if you like, but my roommate tells me their prices are way out of line.

They only have a beer and wine license, and I know how you enjoy your before-dinner martini.

If you had been to that place recently, you would be shocked at how it has gone downhill.

It may have a good cast, but the critic in *Newsweek* says its script, editing, and direction set movies back thirty years.

I make it a point of honor to avoid films that glorify violence.

I caught it at a sneak preview three weeks ago.

I called the ticket office, and they're all sold out.

Frankly, any kind of opera bores me silly.

French ballet is too sissy. Let's wait for the Bolshoi.

Rock festivals wreck my eardrums.

San Francisco used to be a great weekend town, but that was before the crime wave. I wouldn't want to be sniped at while strolling hand in hand up Grant Street in search of Schun Lee Shrimp.

You should never set foot in Las Vegas without at least a fifty-dollar bankroll.

Unless you like being swamped by tourists and standing in hour-long lines, you should take in Disneyland off-season, preferably on a weekday.

The last time I went to Holiday on Ice, I caught a cold.

Go picnicking when rain is predicted?

Sorry, I forgot to bring a lunch basket. Luckily there is a good restaurant close to the park.

Killer sharks are infesting the beaches. It's in all the headlines.

How can I go swimming without my earplugs?

Those ultraviolet rays play hell with this tender skin of mine.

The weatherman predicts a snow alert at 3,000 feet, and I have no tire chains.

They announced a first-stage smog alert. That puts the kibosh on our tennis game.

I just never learned how to roller skate.

Bullfights horrify me.

Boxing ought to be outlawed.

Wrestling is too phony.

The last time I tried to fly a kite in heavy winds like these, I lost it in three minutes.

I hear a chemical plant polluted that lake and killed off all the trout.

I forgot to bring salmon eggs.

I neglected to buy a hunting license.

It's not that I hate seeing your relatives, but the last time I called them they were all coming down with scarlatina.

I'd rather not go if she brings her brother. That boy is always on the make.

As usual they'll insist that I sniff coke with them.

I was there last week. It would be boring to go back so soon.

I couldn't risk driving on the freeway with those worn-out tires.

Why Mine Is Better Than Yours

You mean your group insurance doesn't include dental and psychiatric?

Our firm gets us Buick Rivieras, and they pick up the tab on maintenance and insurance.

My dad, a foreman at General Motors, put my Cutlass together practically by hand, with Cadillac-type insulation, disc-brakes on all four wheels, and the best sports suspension in the business.

I got the dealer to split his profit down the middle, and he threw in all the options at cost and gave me rubber floor mats for nothing.

I'm being cursed with mechanical failures. On Sunday a hose on the Chris-Craft blew out, on Wednesday the Cessna's left engine died, and this morning the Mercedes 450SL started leaking oil. Let's hope the Winnebago holds up long enough to get us to the Rockies.

If you had reminded me, I could've gotten you some great wedding pictures with my new Nikon automatic.

To avoid those glowing eyes you have to bounce your light off the ceiling. Next time borrow my swivel-flash.

If you get sick of looking at commercials, come over and watch a video-cassette of "Rocky" on my big-screen Advent.

My set has detent tuning. Doesn't everybody's?

K-Mart gave us a two-year warranty on ours. You shouldn't have settled for ninety days.

You should subscribe to *Consumer Reports*. This Penney's trenchcoat was a "best buy" and it only cost a third of what you paid for that London Fog.

To add a jacuzzi now will cost you half the original price of your pool. If you had done it when the pool was installed, like I did, you would have gotten it for peanuts. And it's heaven, believe me.

I thought all new houses came with insulated walls and built-in microwave ovens.

Could you use a couple of rakes and an old lawnmower? Our Japanese gardener prefers to bring his own tools, so all that stuff is just collecting rust in our garage.

Thanks for the offer of a loaner, but I'm afraid I would bust a gut if I switched from a magnesium-frame derailleur to an old-fashioned three-speed bike.

Sorry, but I can't stand any blended scotch—not after cracking open that case of single-malt Glenlivit that one of my clients sent me for Christmas.

You wouldn't have those terrible hangovers if you would switch to Beefeater's Gin like I did.

Nice cigar, but would you care for a real Havana? I have a friend in Kuwait who smuggles them out for me.

We just got back from Florence. And how was your week in Wichita?

Sorry we can't join you two for bowling, but my boyfriend just passed his bar exam and he's taking me to The Forum of the Twelve Caesars for the victory dinner.

We'll be a little late. My son lost his Phi Beta Kappa key, and we're all combing through the shag carpet.

Anyone who insulted *my* husband like that would have woken up with a fractured jaw.

I'll pass on that masage parlor. My wife takes care of all my needs.

We're in the same tax bracket as you, and our refund was a thousand dollars more. Next time you had better talk to our tax man.

CHAPTER **25**

The Labyrinthine Excuse

&§ Here, as in one of Rube Goldberg's mechanical mazes, a sense of airtight causality must be sustained from start to finish. And your listener will be convinced even though his willingness to follow all your twists and turns will probably break down somewhere in mid-story—or for that reason especially. After all, how could such a chain of calamities be the deliberate fabrication of anyone but an utter madman?

I took the kids to see "Bambi" at a little theater out in the boonies, and on our way back Jenny kept crying about the death of Bambi's mother and Larry started throwing up from eating too much popcorn and chocolate peppermints. I stopped to comfort them and clean up Larry's mess, and when I tried to restart the car all I got was a click. Since it has an automatic shift and can't be push-started, I figured I'd call the automobile club. The road we were parked on was in the middle of an alfalfa field, but I could see a Shell sign about half a mile away, so we started walking, me carrying Larry the whole distance in that ninety-degree heat. The gas station was closed but it had an outside phone booth and a cold-drink machine. The kids were dying of thirst by now, so I bought them a coke; then with my last remaining dime I called the Triple A. Well, first off, they wanted the number on my plastic membership card, and it was then I realized I had left my wallet in the glove compartment on account of those slim new slacks my wife had bought me which don't have any back pockets. They understood my problem and said they would call my wife and get the number off her duplicate card and also let her know where I was. In the meantime I was supposed to wait for her to call me at the phone booth to confirm the transaction before I returned to my car. Well, twenty minutes passed without a call, and suddenly two cars coming in the opposite direction crashed into each other. The big Chrysler just had a sprung radiator, but the little Datsun was rolled over on its side and gushing smoke like crazy. I ran over to help pull the driver out, and pretty soon the Highway Patrol and a meat wagon were there and I was ordered to stick around to testify as a witness. Meanwhile little Larry began throwing up again, this time violently, so I got the ambulance to take him to the hospital along with the guy in the Datsun, and then I borrowed change from one of the cops to call my wife. Getting no answer, I called our next door neighbor, and she said my wife had gotten a call that her aunt from Munich had arrived a week earlier than scheduled on a special flight, so my wife had taken our old clunker of a Chevy over to the international airport and had called back to have me informed that the old fraulein's luggage was either lost or stolen and the search would take three or four hours. To top that off, the Chevy's clutch had broken down and I was supposed to go out to the airport to pick up both of them. Well, one of the cops took me and Jenny back to the car to start it with his jumper cable, and it turned out that in all the excitement I had locked my keys inside, which necessitated our fooling around with "repo" tools for another fifteen minutes just to get the damn door open. . . .

CHAPTER **26**

Odd Excuses

Unusual

I'm at my French Club. They charge me a quarter for every word they catch me saying in English—so *au revoir, ma cherie.*

Once a year I have a compulsion to update my scrapbook.

I was driving through my old neighborhood and just had to stop off at Sun Yee's Market for some licorice sticks and a slurpy.

I ran into a movie star I worshipped in my adolescence. I asked for her autograph and she was so grateful to be recognized that she asked me to buy her a drink. And then she wanted another one.

Somebody is coming by to make a bid on my collection of old Lucien Lelong perfume bottles.

I wasted the afternoon stripping the paint off a Queen Anne commode I bought at Goodwill for five dollars. It turned out to be Grand Rapids.

My recipe calls for pheasant eggs, and I've been driving all over town trying to find some.

I decided to have my hair styled at Le Gentilhomme. They told me that Ramon would be tied up for at least another hour, and after a forty-minute wait I lost my nerve and went back to Ed's Barber Shop.

I noticed that I'd gained an inch around the waist and realized I hadn't done any jogging in three weeks.

One of the timpels on my gold-rimmed glasses came off, and I've been trying to screw it back on with a pair of tweezers.

Halloween is only a week away, so I was at the costume shop being fitted for an SS uniform.

I saw an eighty-year-old lady trying to load a refrigerator onto a pickup truck. Naturally I stopped to give her a hand.

While I was at the zoo, some man fell over the railing into the wolf compound and got his throat ripped out. What a grisly spectacle! I'm still too traumatized to venture out of the house.

I witnessed a brutal rape and I'm trying to make up my mind to get involved with the police.

Someone left a baby on our doorstep.

You probably called when I was listening to Beethoven's Ninth on my headphones.

It's rare that I find a novel that I *really* can't put down, but this one is it. I'll lend it to you when I'm finished.

My TV set broke down, and I rushed over to K-Mart to catch the end of the movie.

I was shopping in Safeway when a television crew picked me out to do their testimonial for Ivory Liquid. There could be residuals.

What a fool I was to agree to play Polonius with that neighborhood theater group. The director, a hammy old has-been, is one of those tyrant perfectionists who insists on running rehearsals into the wee hours, and I mean every single night! And he treats us like crap. If my boss's wife wasn't their Ophelia, I'd quit the whole deal.

I waited two hours for you to arrive before I realized that I had walked into the wrong New Year's Eve party.

My line has been busy night and day since some malicious idiot scratched my phone number on the wall of the latrine in the men's gym.

Look out for cheap zippers. I was halfway to work when my fly sheared open, and I had to drive back home to put on another pair of pants.

Mystifying

⮜§ Though these excuses are good stalls, they put your listener in such suspense that a full accounting will be doubly mandatory the next time you meet.

Hey, something unexpected came up. I've got to sign off now. I'll give you the whole scoop later.

I'll have to skip that party. One of the people they've invited is a man I don't want to run into. No, I can't tell you who—that would only make it worse. Try to understand.

I don't know where I'll be. I'm waiting for directions.

I couldn't stay home because the telephone keeps ringing and I might have been tempted to answer it.

If I told anyone where I've been, somebody's life could be in danger.

Do you have a bona fide need to know?

I can only tell you that I'm practicing on my autoharp. You'll find out why later.

I've been out all afternoon shopping. It would be a dead give-away if I even told you where I went, let alone what I was looking for. You'll just have to be patient. After all, your birthday is only two months away.

Please don't ask what happened. It was too embarrassing.

You'd never believe it anyway.

(*In a very faint whisper*) I can't talk louder. They'll hear me.

Where am I? Rather ask where are you? Where are we? Where is anybody?

I'm fiddling with my megafilter and may have to take the burbometer over to the fabulator's to be stropped and sized.

Ich werde es später erklären.

Weird

I can't tonight. Mars is in conjunction with Jupiter, which means I would drive recklessly.

The moon is in an adverse aspect with Mercury, and anything I do is bound to get me in trouble.

Last night I dreamed about emeralds, which is always a sign of impending danger. I think I'll just stay home today.

Sorry, but yesterday when I looked at your palm I saw too many breaks in your head line.

I loved the card you sent me, but I'm disturbed by the way you print your capital letters instead of writing them. I never get along with critical, negatively analytical people.

I lost my lucky coin and I go nowhere without it.

I've been hexed.

Drugged

It was that dexie they gave me that made me drink up all the scotch and vodka and hustle every chick at the party and sit up arguing about philosophy till the host and hostess finally crashed at five in the morning. I'll see you in about four hours—just as soon as I get Aristotle's Ethics ironed out with the fry-cook here at Denny's.

Mom, the reason my eyes are so red is because I didn't get home till late last night and had to get up early to mow the lawn in all that smog.

I often forget to read the dosage information on that tube of yellow jackets my doctor prescribed for me, so please don't think I was sore at you when I slugged you and kneed you in the groin.

They salted the potato chips with LSD.

I shouldn't have stayed up so late gluing Billy's model Fokker together without proper ventilation because this morning I'm blind.

As I was walking over that stone bridge in the park I noticed some unusual moss down at the water line. I climbed down there to scrape some off to take to my botany class, and all of a sudden three narcs sprung out of the bushes and handcuffed me. It turned out that that scummy rock was loose and concealed somebody's heroin stash.

Disoriented (Crazy But True)

◄§ Few people who have been swept through the chaos of a traffic accident are equal to the request, "Explain what happened in a few words or less." The following authentic quotes were taken from insurance and accident forms and were later published in the Toronto *Sunday*, July 26, 1977.

Coming home, I drove into the wrong house and collided with a tree I don't have.

The other car collided with mine without giving warning of its intentions.

Thought my window was down but found it was up when I put my hand through it.

Collided with a stationary truck coming the other way.

Truck backed through my windshield into my wife's face.

A pedestrian hit me and went under my car.

The guy was all over the road: had to swerve a number of times before I hit him.

I pulled away from the side of the road. Glanced at my mother-in-law and headed over the embankment.

In an attempt to kill a fly, I drove into a telephone pole.

Had been shopping for plants all day and was on my way home. As I reached an intersection a hedge sprang up obscuring my vision. I did not see the other car.

Had been driving my car for forty years when I fell asleep at the wheel and had my accident.

Was on my way to the doctor's with rear-end trouble when my universal joint gave way causing me to have an accident.

The pedestrian works where I work. He is a standards coordinator. Funny he should be the one I hit.

As I approached the intersection, a stop sign suddenly appeared in a place where no stop sign has ever appeared before. I was unable to stop in time to avoid an accident.

To avoid hitting the bumper of the car in front, I struck the pedestrian.

My car was legally parked as it backed into the other vehicle.

An invisible car came out of nowhere, struck my vehicle, and vanished.

I told the police that I was not injured, but on removing my hat I found that I had a skull fracture.

I was sure the old fellow would never make it to the other side of the roadway when I struck him.

The pedestrian had no idea which direction to go, so I ran over him.

I saw the slow-moving, sad-faced old gentleman as he bounced off my car.

The indirect cause of this accident was a little guy in a small car with a big mouth.

I was thrown from my car as it left the road. I was later found in a ditch by some stray cows.

The telephone pole was approaching fast. I was attempting to swerve out of its path when it struck my front end.

I was unable to stop in time and the car crashed into the other vehicle. The driver and passengers then left immediately for a vacation with injuries.

Honest

Last Saturday I swore I would stop coming to your whingdings until you got yourself a new set of friends.

Frankly, your kids drive me nuts.

I thought it was the thing to do, so I did it.

It's none of your goddamn business why.

I don't want to.

CHAPTER *27*

Dumb Excuses

⋘ Sometimes the razzberry can be better than the best.

I fell asleep and didn't wake up in time to go to bed.

I stopped to watch the sun rise.

The energy crisis has left me too weak to drive my car

I'll tell you what kind of car trouble I had. The driver didn't get into the car in time.

I was delayed for ten minutes at a camel crossing.

The streetcar had a flat tire. (Would you believe it ran out of gas?)

My dogsled broke down and I didn't have a spare dog.

My wife was in the shower when I said goodbye, and it will take awhile for my clothes to dry out.

My wife is going to get pregnant, and I want to be there when it happens.

My wife is hot and I have to stay home and fan her.

I'm meeting Linda Lovelace at Der Wienerschnitzel.

I'm dating an orthodox Jew, so naturally I won't be over for Christmas this year.

I fell down a manhole and the water swept me along for two blocks before I could grab a ladder. When I climbed out I smelled so foul I had to go right back home and take a bath.

Due to the heavy rainstorm, my neighbor's house is blocking my driveway. The house movers won't be here until late afternoon, but by then we expect to have all the debris cleared away, the refugees classified, and the airlift completed.

I feel a cold coming on, and it should be here by twelve noon.

I swallowed my partial plate and I'm waiting for a tracheotomy.

You know that job I got at the City of Hope? Well, they tell me I've been exposed to a massive dose of TB. I'm calling to let you know that I can't come out for ninety days. Besides, my blood-soaked handkerchief would only distract you from your dinner.

My glass eye fell out and rolled behind the refrigerator.

My plant isn't housebroken. It wet the floor and I have to dry the carpet.

I'll need a few minutes to think up a good excuse. Call you back.

CHAPTER **28**

Excuses For Particular People

To the coward: I'd ask you to go hiking with us, but those woods are infested with rattlesnakes.

To the autophobe: Hon, I hesitate to drive even two blocks, let alone the ten miles to your place. My engine has been overheating and now I find I've got a trickly little leak in my gas tank. Probably nothing to worry about unless I get in a collision—then kablooey! (Also see Chapter 3.)

To the skeptical boss: I was about to tell you about my blood pressure, but I figured you wouldn't believe me anyway.

To the swinging boss: Say, Jerry, you're probably wondering why I'm still not in the office. The only excuse I can give you is this fantastic redhead I met at a party last night. Her fiancé was out of town and I mean she had the itch. She invited me over to her apartment and wouldn't let me out of her clutches till dawn.

To the bon vivant: I didn't ask you along because most of the guests were old folks from my mother's church. It was lemonade and cookies all the way.

To the puritan: I didn't think you would enjoy guzzling beer and watching stag films for three hours.

To the gourmet: Their idea of a great entree is mashed potatoes covered with hamburger helper.

To the miser: They always provide two six-packs and then start passing around the kitty.

To the bopper: You wouldn't have enjoyed waltzing to Glen Gray's "Casa Lomans."

To the parent: They live in a tiny apartment, and they don't even own a TV. Your kids would have gone bananas.

To the intellectual: I didn't think you would have anything to say to them.

To the scrawny runt: They always insist that you put on a swimsuit and take a dip in their pool.

To the sexpot: They're too happily married.

To the conservative: When I agreed to meet you I plumb forgot that right after my Marxism seminar I have to hitchhike out to that park where those goons from City Hall are trying to knock over all those fifty-year-old palm trees. I promised some of the guys from my encounter group at Synanon that I'd fill in in front of the bulldozers for an hour or so. Listen, if you're still free later on we could meet at the Self-Realization Fellowship and share a soyburger and then head over to Ralph's to see if his new kilo is all it's cracked up to be.

To the radical: Could we make it the midnight show instead? You see, I'm committed to go to this Ronald Reagan fundraiser out in Anaheim. Hey, you might enjoy it yourself. They will be serving blackberry punch from Knott's Berry Farm and there is always a possibility that George Murphy will show up and do a little tap dance.

CHAPTER *29*

Desperate and Drastic Excuses

◈§ When all else has been tried so many times that you're about as credible as one of Rose Mary Woods's taping gymnastics, when your rich uncle hastily starts revising his will, when your engagement ring comes flying back in your face, when your severance check is about to be rolled into the typewriter—that's desperation time!

My _____ (wife, husband, mother, father, son, daughter) had a massive coronary. I've got to race over to the hospital to sign the papers permitting open-heart surgery.

My _____ had a stroke. Luckily only the right side was paralyzed.

My _____ died today.

I felt sick all night—kind of a tightness in the chest. This morning I woke up with a terrible shooting pain up my left arm. My wife just phoned the paramedics.

I fell down and hit my head on the sidewalk, and now I can't see. That's right, I'm stone blind. My doctor says it's only the temporary effect of a concussion and ought to clear up in a while. I suppose I could come down to the office and give dictation.

I'm starting my first cobalt treatment this afternoon. Ought to be back to work by Wednesday.

Last night I stopped for gas right while the station was being robbed. The two stickup men took me along as a hostage and probably would have snuffed me if they hadn't been rear-ended at a traffic signal, which gave me a second to duck out and start sprinting. I'll be tied up all morning helping the cops to identify the culprits.

My house burned down. It was totaled in twenty minutes, reduced to a heap of smoldering cinders. My God, the cheap materials they put into houses nowadays! The fire inspector tells me it was started by the electric blanket. Anyway, I was lucky to get my family out of there with their lives. Right now I have to contact my insurance agent and then go look for a motel.

The forced-air heater exploded and destroyed half the house. Only one of the kids got hurt.

A small private plane crashed into our living room. You'll probably read about it in the newspaper.

To your D.I. at Marine boot camp: Sir, I wasn't smiling. I had chapped lips and was stretching them.

Making love?—you're kidding! She had a heart seizure and I was trying to give mouth-to-mouth resuscitation.

CHAPTER 30

Famous Excuses

In Their Own Words

The woman whom thou gavest to be with me, she gave me of the tree, and I did eat.

ADAM

The serpent beguiled me, and I did eat.

EVE

For I disobeyed, not from a better choice, but from love of play, loving the pride of victory in my contests, and to have my ears tickled with lying fables, that they might itch the more.

ST. AUGUSTINE

I have unveiled my inmost self even as Thou hast seen it, O Eternal Being. Gather round me the countless host of my fellow-men; let them hear my confessions, lament for my unworthiness, and blush for my imperfections. Then let each of them in turn reveal, with the same frankness, the secrets of his heart at the foot of the Throne, and say, if he dare, *"I was better than that man!"*

JEAN-JACQUES ROUSSEAU

The only way to get rid of temptation is to yield to it.

OSCAR WILDE

There is no great genius without some touch of madness.

SENECA

I was going home two hours ago, but was met by Mr. Griffith, who has kept me ever since. I will come within a pint of wine.

The finest woman in nature should not detain me an hour from you; but you must sometimes suffer the rivalship of the wisest men.

A little in drink, but at all times yr. faithfull husband.

SIR RICHARD STEELE, Letters to His Wife

Again I must complain of Indolence: she is a tyrant who oppresses me, who confines me in bed as criminals are confined in their cells. In vain I try to rise. I am weighed down with the heaviest of fetters. I have freedom of motion only to stretch my legs and fold my arms; my very eyes appear to be held shut with fine chains. What witchcraft!

JAMES BOSWELL

Were he not to marry again, it might be concluded that his first wife had given him a disgust to marriage; but by taking a second wife he pays the highest compliment to the first, by showing that she made him so happy as a married man, that he wishes to be so a second time.

[He] is dull, naturally dull; but it must have taken him a great deal of pains to become what we now see him. Such an excess of stupidity, sir, is not in Nature.

SAMUEL JOHNSON

Order, with regard to places for things, papers, etc., I found extremely difficult to acquire. I had not been early accustomed to it, and, having an exceeding good memory, I was not so sensible of the inconvenience attending want of method.

BENJAMIN FRANKLIN

There is the greatest practical benefit in making a few failures early in life.

THOMAS HENRY HUXLEY

My Dear Lady Holland,
 I have not the heart, when an amiable lady says,
"Come to Semiramis *in my box," to decline; but I get*

bolder at a distance. Semiramis *would be to me pure misery. I love music very little—I hate acting; I have the worst opinion of Semiramis herself, and the whole thing (I cannot help it) seems so childish and foolish that I cannot abide it. Moreover it would be rather out of etiquette for a Canon of St. Paul's to go to an opera, and where etiquette prevents me from doing things disagreeable to myself, I am a perfect martinet. All these things considered, I am sure you will not be a* Semiramis *to me, but let me off.*

REVEREND SYDNEY SMITH

The walking-stick serves the purpose of an advertisement that the bearer's hands are employed otherwise than in useful effort, and it therefore has utility as an evidence of leisure.

THORSTEIN VEBLEN

I am from Missouri. You have got to show me.

WILLARD D. VANDIVER

All I know is just what I read in the papers.

WILL ROGERS

I've made it a rule never to drink by daylight and never to refuse a drink after dark.

H. L. MENCKEN

Dear Lawrence [Durrell],

I forgot to think you for the pound, crisper than celery and sweeter than sugar oh the lovely sound, not through ingratitude, it's as welcome as a woman is cleft, but through work (half a poem about energy), sloth (in a chair looking at my feet or the mirror or unread novels or counting the patterns on the floor to see if I can work out a system for my football pools or watching my wife knit or dance), depression (because, mostly, there weren't more pounds from more people), small habits (from bar-billiards to broadcast talks, slick bonneted Hampshire roadhouses and so-cialist teas), love, unqualified, the nearness of Bourne-mouth, colds and pains in the head and your Black

197 . . .

*Book about which more in another and longer
letter. . . .*

DYLAN THOMAS*

For sixteen years I lived . . . distrusting the rich, yet working
for money with which to share their mobility and the grace that
some of them brought into their lives. During this time I had plenty
of the usual horses shot from under me—I remember some of their
names—*Punctured Pride, Thwarted Expectation, Faithless, Show-
off, Hard Hit, Never Again.* And after a while I wasn't twenty-five,
then not even thirty-five, and nothing was quite as good.

F. SCOTT FITZGERALD

Only excuse for this tired death route is THE KICK when the
junk circuit is cut off for the nonpayment and the junk-skin dies of
junk-lack and overdose of time and the Old Skin has forgotten the
skin game simplifying a way under the junk cover the way skins
will. . . . A condition of total exposure is precipitated when the
Kicking Addict cannot chose but see smell and listen. . . . Watch
out for the cars.

WILLIAM BURROUGHS

The car overturned in a deep pond and immediately filled with
water. I remember thinking as the cold water rushed in around my
head that I was, for certain, drowning. But somehow I struggled to
the surface alive. I made immediate and repeated efforts to save
Mary Jo by diving into the strong and murky current, but succeeded only in increasing my state of utter exhaustion and alarm.

SENATOR EDWARD M. KENNEDY

I couldn't do a show where I just sing songs dressed in normal
clothes Anybody can do that.

ALICE COOPER

THE AMERICAN INDIAN

I am sorry to hear that the Indians have commenced war, but
greatly pleased you have been so decisive on that head. Nothing
will reduce those wretches so soon as pushing the war into the heart
of their country. But I would not stop there. I would never cease

* Fitzgibbon, Constantine, ed. *Selected Letters of Dylan Thomas.* New York:
New Directions Books. Copyright © 1965, 1966 by the Trustees for the Copy-
rights of Dylan Thomas, pp. 223-224.

pursuing them while one of them remained on this side of the Mississippi. . . . The Indians are a useless, expensive, ungovernable ally.

THOMAS JEFFERSON, 1776

The only good Indians I ever saw were dead.

GENERAL PHILIP H. SHERIDAN, 1869

It is probably true that the majority of our wild Indians have no inherited tendencies whatever toward morality or chastity, according to an enlightened standard. Chastity and morality among them must come from education and contact with the better element of the whites.

W. A. JONES, COMMISSIONER OF INDIAN AFFAIRS, 1903

SLAVERY

The slaves. Although he was in a state of slavery, the Negro of plantation days was usually happy. He was fond of the company of others and liked to sing, dance, crack jokes, and laugh; he admired bright colors and was proud to wear a red or yellow bandana. He wanted to be praised, and he was loyal to a kind master or overseer. He was never in a hurry, and was always ready to let things go until the morrow. Most of the planters learned that not the whip, but loyalty, based upon pride, kindness, and rewards, brought the best returns.

THOMAS MARSHALL'S *American History,* 1930

LEADERS AND MISLEADERS

I am afraid of nothing. I shall roast you over the coals for calling me afraid!

What is the throne?—a bit of wood gilded and covered with velvet. I am the state—I alone am here the representative of the people. Even if I had done wrong you should not have reproached me in public—people wash their dirty linen at home. France has more need of me than I of France.

IVAN THE TERRIBLE

A great reputation is a great noise. The greater noise you make, the farther off you are heard. Laws, institutions, monuments, nations, all fall. But the noise continues and resounds in after ages.

NAPOLEON BONAPARTE

England expects every man to do his duty.

HORATIO NELSON

It is humiliating to remain with our hands folded while others write history. It matters little who wins. To make a people great, it is necessary to send them into battle even if you have to kick them in the pants. This is what I shall do.

It was useless to attempt to blaze a trail by fine words, by sermons from chairs. It was necessary to give timely, genial recognition to chivalrous violence.

(On the forced flight of the Italian Army from its Albania base, Koritza) The rugged mountains and the muddy valleys of that country are not adapted to our kind of fighting.

BENITO MUSSOLINI

All our fifth columnists have been liquidated in the purge.

JOSEF STALIN, 1938

Mankind has grown strong in eternal struggles and it will only perish through eternal peace.

If this earth really has room enough for all to live in, then one should give us the space that we need for living.

I have said and done all that I could; I have made proposal after proposal to Britain; likewise to France. These proposals were always ridiculed—rejected with scorn. However, when I saw that the other side intended to fight, I naturally . . . forged a powerful weapon of defense.

ADOLF HITLER

What? Pity your less fortunate fellow men? Absurd! My young friend, away with all sentimentality! Don't be ashamed of your strength. Let others be ashamed of their weakness. If you want to enjoy an omelette you must be willing to break the eggs. If you want to grow in the sun you must be ready to thrust your fellows into the shadow. Indeed, your own good fortune *depends* upon the misfortune of everybody else. . . . Live, but don't let live.

WILHELM VAN WULFEN, *The Man Of Lust* (a Hitler favorite)

I have found it impossible to carry the heavy burden of responsibility and to discharge my duties as King as I would wish to do without the help and support of the woman I love.

THE DUKE OF WINSOR (EDWARD VIII)

As Chinese troops have recently shown frequent signs of movements along the northern frontier of French Indo-China bordering on China, Japanese troops with the object of mainly taking precautionary measures, have been reinforced to a certain extent in the northern part of French Indo-China. As a natural sequence of this step, certain movements have been made among the troops stationed in the southern part of the said territory. It seems that an exaggerated report has been made of these movements.

MESSAGE FROM THE JAPANESE AMBASSADOR TO THE U.S.
SECRETARY OF STATE, December 5, 1941

I shall return.

GENERAL DOUGLAS MACARTHUR, 1942

I'm the only President you've got.

LYNDON BAINES JOHNSON

THE GREAT DEPRESSION

Nobody is actually starving. The hoboes, for example, are better fed than they have ever been. One hobo in New York got ten meals in one day.

PRESIDENT HERBERT HOOVER, 1932

Why, it's the best education in the world for those boys, that traveling around! They get more experience in a few months than they would in years at school.

HENRY FORD

Why, I've never thought of paying men on the basis of what they need. I pay for efficiency. Personally, I attend to all those other things, social welfare stuff, in my church work.

J. E. EDGERTON, PRESIDENT OF THE
NATIONAL ASSOCIATION OF MANUFACTURERS

Many of the bad effects of the so-called Depression are based on calamity howling.

A SPOKESMAN FOR THE NATIONAL ASSOCIATION OF MANUFACTURERS

The banks of the country are generally in a strong position.

SECRETARY OF COMMERCE THOMAS LAMONT

Leaping lizards! Who said business is bad?

LITTLE ORPHAN ANNIE

Wasn't the Depression terrible?
A 1931 SLOGAN SEEN ON BILLBOARDS RENTED BY ADMIRERS OF
PRESIDENT HOOVER

CROOKS AND OTHERS

A mystic force armed my hand. I had no reason at all to kill
President Doumer. On the train to Paris I struggled against my
idea of committing the crime. Then I drank an entire bottle of
cognac. I was too intoxicated to remember what I did.

DR. PAUL GORGULOV, ASSASSIN

Gentlemen, to find Lizzie Borden guilty you must believe that
she is a fiend. Does she look it? The prisoner at the bar is a woman,
and a Christian woman, the equal of your wife and mine.

THE ATTORNEY FOR THE DEFENSE

Q. By "Ben" you mean Ben Siegel?

A. Yes; and he gave me some money, too; bought me a house
in Florida. And then I used to bet horses. . . . I don't know if it is
right or wrong. I paid income tax on that. That money, I used to
save it. When I am supposed to be out giving these parties, it was
fellows that I was going with. They paid for things that I did. I
didn't pay for it. If I was paying for it, I wouldn't have gone in the
first place. After all, I didn't have to give my own parties, I don't
think. But I have never had any businesses in my life. Whatever I
ever had was, outside of betting horses, was given to me.

VIRGINIA HILL (GIRL FRIEND OF SLAIN MOBSTER
BUGGSY SIEGEL) TO THE KEFAUVER COMMITTEE

Now Bonnie and Clyde are the Barrow gang.
I'm sure you all have read
How they rob and steal
And those who squeal
Are usually found dying or dead.

There's lots of untruths to these write-ups;
They're not so ruthless as that;
Their nature is raw;
They hate all the law—
The stool pigeons, spotters and rats.

They call them cold-blooded killers;
They say they are heartless and mean;

But I say this with pride
That I once knew Clyde
When he was honest and upright and clean.

But the laws fooled around,
Kept taking him down
And locking him up in a cell,
Till he said to me
"I'll never be free,
So I'll meet a few of them in hell."
BONNIE PARKER, *From "The Story Of Bonnie and Clyde"*

You know, you just keep putting a little snow on top of snow
and pretty soon it's going to break. Jimmy wanted to be a man.
THE MOTHER OF MARK ESSEX, STATING HER SON'S REASON FOR
KILLING NINE AND WOUNDING NINE IN NEW ORLEANS

In our history books we pay tribute to the man with the gun.
He won the American Revolution and the War of 1812. He de-
fended democracy in 1917–18. He fought the greatest global war in
history in 1941–45. The American with a gun has been a great
stabilizing influence in maintaining a balance of world power.
Between the wars, the National Rifle Association has been the primary guardian of the American rifleman tradition which becomes
so vital in time of war.
SPOKESMAN FOR THE NATIONAL RIFLE ASSOCIATION

Why should I be ashamed? I never took anything to help
myself. I was merely collecting political contributions, and even
then, I wasn't collecting them directly, the way some of the testi-
monies say.
SPIRO T. AGNEW

I never in my life wanted to be left behind.
RICHARD M. NIXON

ON DEWEY'S UNEXPECTED DEFEAT
BY TRUMAN IN 1948
We were too isolated with other reporters; and we, too, were
far too impressed by the tidy statistics of the poll.
JAMES RESTON

I don't know what happened.
GEORGE GALLUP

A MALFUNCTION

I passed all the other courses that I took at my University, but I could never pass botany. This was because all botany students had to spend several hours a week in a laboratory looking through a microscope at plant cells, and I could never see through a microscope. I never once saw a cell through a microscope. This used to enrage my instructor. He would wander around the laboratory pleased with the progress all the students were making in drawing the involved and, so I am told, interesting structure of flower cells, until he came to me. I would just be standing there. "I can't see anything," I would say. He would begin patiently enough, explaining how anybody can see through a microscope, but he would always end up in a fury, claiming that I could *too* see through a microscope but just pretended that I couldn't. "It takes away from the beauty of flowers anyway," I used to tell him. "We are not concerned with beauty in this course," he would say. "We are concerned solely with what I may call the *mechanics* of flars." "Well," I'd say, "I can't see anything." "Try it just once again," he'd say, and I would put my eye to the microscope and see nothing at all, except now and again a nebulous milky substance—a phenomenon of maladjustment. You were supposed to see a vivid, restless clockwork of sharply defined plant cells. "I see what looks like a lot of milk," I would tell him. This, he claimed, was the result of my not having adjusted the microscope properly, so he would readjust it for me, or rather, for himself. And I would look again and see milk.

JAMES THURBER, "University Days"*

A WARNING

There is an epigram in *Martial* . . . in which he humorously tells the story of Coelius, who pretended to have the gout to avoid paying court to some of the great in Rome, being present at their levee, and attending and following them; and, to make his excuse more plausible, had his legs anointed and swathed, and counterfeited completely the carriage and bearing of a gouty man. In the end fortune gave him the pleasure of making him so in fact:

> So much can skill and effort bring about:
> Coelius no longer feigns, but has, the gout.
> —*Martial*

MICHEL DE MONTAIGNE

From Literature

Love, which in gentlest hearts will soonest bloom
    seized my lover with passion for that sweet body
    from which I was torn unshriven to my doom.

Love, which permits no loved one not to love,
    took me so strongly with delight in him
    that we are one in Hell, as we were above.
              DANTE, *The Inferno* (Francesca's Story)

I bought three kerchers to thy head,
    That were wrought fine and gallantly:
I kept thee both at board and bed,
    Which cost my purse well favouredly.

I bought thee petticoats of the best,
    The cloth so fine as fine might be:
I gave thee jewels for thy chest,
    And all this cost I spent on thee.

Thy gown was of the grassy green,
    Thy sleeves of satin hanging by:
Which made thee be our harvest queen
    And yet thou wouldst not love me.
              ANONYMOUS, "Greensleeves"

Ah, take the Cash, and let the credit go,
Nor heed the rumble of a distant drum.
    While you live,
Drink!—for, once dead, you never shall return.
              OMAR KHAYYAM, *The Rubáiyát*

WILLIAM SHAKESPEARE:
Since I cannot be a lover,
To entertain these fair well-spoken days,
I am determined to prove a villain
And hate the idle pleasures of these days.
              Richard III, Act I

I hate the Moor,
And it is thought abroad that 'twixt my sheets
He has done my office: I know not if 't be true,
But I, for mere suspicion in that kind,
Will do as if for surety.

Othello, Act I

I love bastards: I am a bastard begot, bastard instructed, bastard in mind, bastard in valour, in every thing illegitimate.

Troilus and Cressida, Act V

I have often heard my mother say
I came into the world with my legs forward.

III Henry VI, Act V

I am a very foolish fond old man,
Fourscore and upward, not an hour more nor less;
And, to deal plainly,
I fear I am not in my perfect mind.

King Lear, Act IV

Read not my blemishes in the world's report:
I have not kept my square; but that to come
Shall all be done by the rule.

Antony and Cleopatra, Act II

How hard it is for women to keep counsel!

Julius Caesar, Act II

I thought all for the best.

Romeo and Juliet, Act III

Our will and fates do so contrary run
That our devices still are overthrown.

Hamlet, Act III

Conscience doth make cowards of us all.

Hamlet, Act III

Certainly my conscience will serve me to run from this Jew, my
master. The fiend is at mine elbow and tempts me saying to me,

... 'Good Launcelot, ... use your legs, take the start, run away.'
... My conscience says 'Launcelot, budge not.' 'Budge,' says the
fiend ... The fiend gives more friendly counsel: I will run.

The Merchant of Venice, Act II

I am but shadow of myself:
You are deceived, my substance is not here.

I Henry VI, Act II

I am a man
More sinn'd against than sinning.

King Lear, Act III

I have an answer that will serve all men. ... It is like a barber's
chair that fits all buttocks.

All's Well that Ends Well, Act II

King: *Teach us, sweet madam, for our rude*
transgression
Some fair excuse.
Princess: *The fairest is confession.*

Love's Labour's Lost, Act V

Out upon it, I have loved
Three whole days together;
And am like to love three more,
If it prove fair weather.

JOHN SUCKLING, "Constancy"

I could not love thee, dear, so much,
Lov'd I not honour more.

RICHARD LOVELACE, "To Lucasta"

But at my back I always hear
Time's winged chariot hurrying near;
And yonder all before us lie
Deserts of vast eternity.

ANDREW MARVELL, "To His Coy Mistress"

My valour is certainly going! it is sneaking off! I feel it oozing
out, as it were, at the palm of my hands!

RICHARD BRINSLEY SHERIDAN, *The Rivals, Act V*

Here's to the maiden of bashful fifteen;
  Here's to the widow of fifty;
Here's to the flaunting, extravagant quean,
  And here's to the housewife that's thrifty!
    Let the toast pass;
    Drink to the lass;
I'll warrant she'll prove an excuse for the glass.
                SHERIDAN, *The School for Scandal, Act I*

"But what good came of it at last?"
Quoth little Peterkin.
"Why that I cannot tell," said he;
"But 'twas a famous victory."
                ROBERT SOUTHEY, "The Battle of Blenheim"

With lips unbrightened, wreathless brow, I stroll:
And would you learn the spells that drowse my soul?
Work without Hope draws nectar in a sieve,
And Hope without an object cannot live.
                S. T. COLERIDGE, "Work Without Hope"

I asked a thief to steal me a peach,
He turned up his eyes;
I asked a lithe lady to lie her down,
Holy & meek she cries.

As soon as I went
An angel came
He wink'd at the thief
And smiled at the dame—

And without one word said
Had a peach from the tree
And still as a maid
Enjoy'd the lady.
                WILLIAM BLAKE, "I Asked a Thief"

Who does not love wine, women, and song
Remains a fool his whole life long.
                JOHANN H. VOSS, "Wine, Women and Song"

I haven't the gift of gab, my sons—because
I'm bred to the sea.
FREDERICK MARRYAT, "The Old Navy"

I'm no angel.

I think I could be a good woman if I had five thousand a year.
WILLIAM MAKEPEACE THACKERAY, *Vanity Fair*

Remember, it's as easy to marry a rich woman as a poor woman.
THACKERAY, *Pendennis*

CHARLES DICKENS:
It is at least as difficult to stay a moral infection as a physical one.

Little Dorrit

Regrets are the natural property of gray hairs.
Martin Chuzzlewit

I am a lorn creetur . . . and everythink goes contrairy with me.
David Cooperfield

Annual income twenty pounds, annual expenditure nineteen nineteen six, result happiness. Annual income twenty pounds, annual expenditure twenty pounds ought and six, result misery.
David Copperfield

And I *do* come home at Christmas. We all do, or we all should. We all come home, or ought to come home, for a short holiday— the longer, the better—from the great boarding-school, where we are forever working at our arithmetical slates, to take, and give a rest.
"A Christmas Tree"

It is a far, far better thing that I do, than I have ever done; it is a far, far better rest that I go to, than I have ever known.
A Tale of Two Cities

Please, sir, I want some more.
Oliver Twist

"You are old, Father William," the young man said,
   "And your hair has become very white;
And yet you incessantly stand on your head—
   Do you think, at your age it is right?"

"In my youth," Father William replied to his son,
   "I feared it might injure the brain;
But, now that I'm perfectly sure I have none,
   Why, I do it again and again."

"You are old," said the youth, as I mentioned before,
   And have grown most uncommonly fat;
Yet you turned a back-somersault in at the door—
   Pray, what is the reason for that?"

"In my youth," said the sage, as he shook his grey
      locks,
   "I kept all my limbs very supple.
By the use of this ointment—one shilling a box—
   Allow me to sell you a couple?"

"You are old," said the youth, "and your jaws are
      too weak
   For anything tougher than suet;
Yet you finished the goose, with the bones and
      the beak—
   Pray, how did you manage to do it?"

"In my youth," said his father, "I took to the law,
   And argued each case with my wife;
And the muscular strength, which it gave to my jaw,
   Has lasted the rest of my life."

"You are old," said the youth, "one would hardly
      suppose
   That your eye was as steady as ever;
Yet you balanced an eel on the end of your nose—
   What made you so awfully clever?"

"I have answered three questions, and that is enough,"
   Said his father. "Don't give yourself airs!
Do you think I can listen all day to such stuff!
   Be off, or I'll kick you down stairs!"
                          LEWIS CARROLL, "Father William"
                   From Alice's Adventures in Wonderland

He has the luck to be unhampered by either character, or con-
viction, or social position; so that Liberalism is the easiest thing in
the world for him.

HENRIK IBSEN, *The League of Youth*

A nap, my friend, is a brief period of sleep which overtakes
superannuated persons when they endeavor to entertain unwelcome
visitors or to listen to scientific lectures.

GEORGE BERNARD SHAW, *Back to Methuselah*

Some keep the Sabbath going to church;
I keep it staying at home,
With a bobolink for a chorister,
And an orchard for a dome.

EMILY DICKINSON, "A Service of Song"

And a woman is only a woman, but a good cigar is
a smoke.

RUDYARD KIPLING, "The Betrothed"

Nor law, nor duty bade me fight,
Nor public men, nor cheering crowds,
A lonely impulse of delight
Drove to this tumult in the clouds.

W. B. YEATS, "An Irish Airman Foresees His Death"

Two roads diverged in a wood, and I—
I took the one less travelled by,
And that has made all the difference.

ROBERT FROST, "The Road Not Taken"

No! I am not Prince Hamlet, nor was meant to be;
Am an attendant lord, one that will do
To swell a progress, start a scene or two,
Advise the prince; no doubt, an easy tool,
Deferential, glad to be of use,
Politic, cautious, and meticulous;
Full of high sentence, but a bit obtuse;
At times, indeed, almost ridiculous—
Almost, at times, the Fool.

T. S. ELIOT, "The Love Song of J. Alfred Prufrock"

I couldn't find the food I liked. If I had found it, believe me, I should have made no fuss and stuffed myself like you or anyone else.

FRANZ KAFKA, "A Hunger Artist"

I forget who it was that recommended men for their soul's good to do each day two things they disliked: . . . it is a precept that I have followed scrupulously; for every day I have got up and I have gone to bed.

W. SOMERSET MAUGHAM, *The Moon and Sixpence*

Thank heavens, the sun has gone in, and I don't have to go out and enjoy it.

LOGAN PEARSALL SMITH, *Afterthoughts*

My candle burns at both ends;
It will not last the night;
But, ah, my foes, and, oh, my friends—
It gives a lovely light.
EDNA ST. VINCENT MILLAY, *A Few Figs From Thistles*, "First Fig"

Home is heaven and orgies are vile,
But I like an orgy, once in a while.
OGDEN NASH, "Home, 99 44/100% Sweet Home"

When the bank refused to lend Feitelman ten thousand dollars on a risky real-estate venture, he went to call on his lodge brother, the big cloak-and-suiter Hyamson, as a last resort.

"Hyamson, my friend," he said, "I've come to ask you to lend me ten thousand dollars."

Hyamson nodded politely, reflectively puffed on his cigar, but didn't answer.

Thinking he hadn't heard him correctly the first time, Feitelman repeated his request. Still Hyamson didn't answer.

Finally, exasperated Feitelman burst out, "Why don't you say something, Hyamson? You owe me an answer at least."

Slowly Hyamson took the cigar out of his mouth. Looking intently at Feitelman he said, "Sure, Feitelman, I owe you an answer. But better I should owe you an answer than that you should owe me ten thousand dollars."

A TREASURY OF JEWISH HUMOR

A million million spermatozoa,
  All of them alive:
Out of their cataclysm but one poor Noah
  Dare hope to survive.
And among that billion minus one
  Might have chanced to be
Shakespeare, another Newton, a new Donne—
  But the One was Me.
                    ALDOUS HUXLEY, "Fifth Philosopher's Song"

"It isn't fun any more."

He was afraid to look at Marjorie. Then he looked at her. She sat there with her back towards him. He looked at her back. "It isn't fun any more. Not any of it."

She didn't say anything. He went on. "I feel as though everything was gone to hell inside me. I don't know, Marge. I don't know what to say."

He looked on at her back.

"Isn't love any fun?" Marjorie said.

"No," Nick said.

                    ERNEST HEMINGWAY, "The End of Something"

All animals are equal, but some animals are more equal than others.

                    GEORGE ORWELL, *Animal Farm*

From the Movies

I met you ten years too late.

        Tom Brown (Gary Cooper) in *Morocco*, 1930

Where should we be if nobody tried to find out what lies beyond?

        Dr. Henry Frankenstein (Colin Clive) in *Frankenstein*, 1931

I ain't so tough.

        Tom Powers (James Cagney) in *The Public Enemy*, 1931

It took more than one man to change my name to Shanghai Lily!

        Shanghai Lily (Marlene Dietrich) in *Shanghai Express*, 1932

I'm the finest woman who ever walked the streets.
>Lady Lou (Mae West) in *She Done Him Wrong*, 1933

Frankie! Frankie! Your mother forgives me!
>Gypo Nolan (Victor McLaglen) in *The Informer*, 1935

I ain't very much, but I'se all I got.
>Noah (Eddie Anderson) in *The Green Pastures*, 1936

Oh, I'm eternally right. But what good does it do me?
>Alan Squier (Leslie Howard) in *The Petrified Forest*, 1936

What does it matter if an individual is shattered if only Justice is resurrected?
>Zola (Paul Muni) in *The Life of Emile Zola*, 1937

Do you think they'd let me win?—the fates, the destinies, whoever they are who decide what we do or don't get? They've been at me now nearly a quarter of a century. No letup. First they said, "Let him do without parents. He'll get along." Then they decided, "He doesn't need any education. That's for sissies." Then right at the beginning they tossed a coin: "Heads he's poor, tails he's rich." So they tossed a coin—with two heads.
>Mickey Borden (John Garfield) in *Four Daughters*, 1938

There is no such thing as a bad boy.
>Father Flanagan (Spencer Tracy) in *Boy's Town*, 1938

After all, tomorrow is another day!
>Scarlett O'Hara (Vivien Leigh) in *Gone With the Wind*, 1939

Frankly, my dear, I don't give a damn!
>Rhett Butler (Clark Gable) in *Gone With the Wind*

You've nothing to stay for. You've nothing to live for, really, have you. Look down there. It's easy, isn't it. Why don't you?
>Mrs. Danvers (Judith Anderson) in *Rebecca*, 1940

When a man's partner is killed, he's supposed to do something about it. It doesn't make any difference what you thought of him. He was your partner, and you're supposed to do something about it.
>Sam Spade (Humphrey Bogart) in *The Maltese Falson*, 1941

I'm only a poor corrupt official.
Captain Louis Renault (Claude Rains) in *Casablanca*, 1942

Don't ask for the moon when we have the stars.
Charlotte Vale (Bette Davis) in *Now Voyager*, 1942

I don't know how to kiss or I would kiss you. Where do the noses go?
Maria (Ingrid Bergman) in *For Whom the Bell Tolls*, 1943

I never worry about anything that happens to a woman.
Rocklin (John Wayne) in *Tall in the Saddle*, 1941

He's always mean to me. He treats me like dirt.
Phyllis Dietrichson (Barbara Stanwyck) in *Double Indemnity*, 1941

Mass killing. Does not the world encourage it? I am only an amateur by comparison.
Henri Verdoux (Charles Chaplin) in *Monsieur Verdoux*, 1947

In these days, old man, nobody thinks in terms of human beings. Governments don't, so why should we? They talk of the people and the proletariat, and I talk of the mugs. It's the same thing. They have their five year plans and so have I.
Harry Lime (Orson Welles) in *The Third Man*, 1947

Rocco wants *more!*
Johnny Rocco (Edward G. Robinson) in *Key Largo*, 1948

One Rocco more or less isn't worth dying for.
Frank McCloud (Humphrey Bogart), in *Key Largo*

I'm still big. It's the pictures that got small.
Norma Desmond (Gloria Swanson) in *Sunset Boulevard*, 1950

I could have had class. I could have been a contender. Charley, you should have looked out for me.
Terry Malloy (Marlon Brando) in *On the Waterfront*, 1954

Nobody's perfect.
Osgood Fielding (Joe E. Brown) in *Some Like It Hot*, 1959

Gentlemen, you can't fight in here. This is the War Room!
President Merkin Muffley (Peters Sellers) in *Dr. Strangelove: Or
How I Learned to Stop Worrying and Love the Bomb*, 1964

The bottom is loaded with nice people. Only cream and bastards rise.

Lee Harper (Paul Newman) in *Harper*, 1966

I can't beat him. But that don't bother me. The only thing I want to do is go the distance, that's all. Because if that bell rings and I'm still standing, then I'm gonna know for the first time in my life, see, that I weren't just another bum from the neighborhood.

Rocky Balboa (Sylvester Stallone) in *Rocky*, 1976

AFTERWORD

How This Book Came to Be

◆§ My personal interest in excuses began four years ago when, as a college English instructor, I was assigned a class in creative writing. After a fairly slow start with some exercises in description, I came upon a statement by John O'Hara: "A novelist lies to tell the truth." I had to agree with that. If imaginative thinking was my subject, what better test of it than a lie—or *excuse*—designed to convince others through its fidelity to everyday probabilities, its psychological plausibility, and its subtleties of nuance? I set up a few basic categories such as "calling in sick," "breaking a date," and "bugging out of chores," and I asked my students to write out what they considered their own surefire standbys. They responded delightedly, and the vigorous cross-examining that followed each attempt furnished a sound basis for much of the story critiquing that was to become the heart of the course. Not only that, we got a lot of laughs from that exercise. There was something that loved excuses qua excuses—viewed as little pennants of human defiance.

During that semester one of my best friends, Leon W., who had heard about my excuses project, approached me with a personal problem. Here, in slightly edited form, was his explanation:

"When we first bought that tract house in Magnolia Heights we were looking forward to some pleasant social experiences. You know, those gracious suburban get-togethers with toddies and canapés. But four months went by and the right kind of neighbors just didn't turn up. Then one night we met the Fultons and we really seemed to hit it off. Joe and I were both UCLA graduates,

Democrats, and amateur photographers, and his wife Peggy shared Mary's enthusiasm for bonzais. Also our kids all went to the same school. And to really top it off, Joe turned out to be the nephew of my supervisor!

"Well, it wasn't long before they invited us over for some martinis and 'finger foods.' It was a nifty evening of small talk, climaxed most interestingly when my boss dropped in and stuck around for a drink and gave me some rather confidential inside dope on recent events in our office. I was flattered since up to then I'd often wondered if he even knew my name.

"The next weekend we had the Fultons over to our place, and at the end of that session some mention was made of our getting together the following Saturday for bowling, but I had to pass on it as some unexpected expenses had put us on a tight budget and I'd need a couple of free days to tackle a moonlight account I'd taken on. Well, Saturday came and no sooner did I start to work than the phone rang and it was Joe Fulton begging me for a little assistance in hauling a large bookcase out his front door. I said okay and drove right over, and imagine how surprised I was to discover that he had just bought another house a block away and was in the process of moving all his belongings by himself. Well, I felt obliged to lend a hand, especially since his car had broken down and I drive a big wagon, and thus my brief errand turned into five hours of coolie labor. At the end of the moving stint, he and Peggy insisted that we take a raincheck for dinner the Friday next. 'A housewarming, okay?'

"Dinner turned out to be a Colonel Sander's bucket on a dutch-treat basis followed by my spending three hours helping them figure out the 'easy installation' instructions for their new garbage disposal, hanging lamps and curtain rods. However, that evening did end on one pleasant note—we agreed to start babysitting each other's kids, thus saving ourselves lots of money.

"On Monday we learned that our end of the bargain was all go: Joe's half-yearly vacation was upon him and they had made reservations at the MGM Grand Hotel in Las Vegas. So for four days we had their son and daughter on our hands. Except for Joe Jr.'s insulin shots and Libby's daily trip to the therapist ten miles away and a few bloody confrontations between them and our kids, it wasn't all that bad.

"By now you can see the pattern that was emerging and can understand why, when the phone began jingling soon after the Fulton's return, I urged Mary, 'Let it ring! Forget it!' But it persisted and I had to give in. 'Hi, this is Joe.' 'Hello, Joe.' 'Say, how does it look for July Fourth? We're having a barbecue complete with poolside fireworks, so bring the kiddies.' 'Well, er, uh, the boy has a bad cold.' 'No problem, our kids have colds too so they can't affect each other. And a heated pool in the summer is the best therapy in the world. Besides, your boss will be there and he'll be sorry if you don't show.'

"Again I relented. And I have to admit that, apart from the fact that my boss never arrived and most of the beers and roman candles were the ones I brought, it was a pretty enjoyable Fourth after all. In fact, we've had several other good days with the Fultons, sandwiched in between those lousy kind, and recently they mentioned repaying that babysitting favor so that we can take a few days' second honeymoon. Now that's a deal we'd dearly love if our bills weren't piling up so fast.

"So there you have it—the bind we're in. I mean, one more unplanned bucket or fifth of booze or bowling-alley tab and we're skirting ruin . . . unless I can keep my weekends free for moonlighting, which has become impossible. Often I feel like telling the Fultons to shove it for keeps. But then every time I run into my supervisor, he asks me how Joe is doing. It's like I'm almost a member of the family myself, and I see a hint of a promotion on the horizon. And there *is* that second honeymoon possibility. So I'm stuck with trying to weasle out of two out of three Fulton summonses, which, by the way, never cease.

"The trouble is I'm not doing too well at it. The moment the phone rings, all intelligent dodges flee me. I keep using vague off-the-wall crap like that kid's cold or 'car problems' or 'I'm under the weather,' and they've always got a very logical counter-suggestion. I mean, if I didn't respond it would be just the same as telling them to shove it. So I've come to you for some advice."

Leon's plight touched me deeply both on a personal level and as a technical problem. The relationship he had described seemed a classic balance of plusses and minuses, unamenable to the kind of major tampering that would queer the whole deal, yet in dire need of relays and bypasses. In other words, a typical real-life situation.

In answer to his plea I dug out my batch of student excuses and went to my desk and typed a few of the best ones onto a single sheet. My advice was to study them carefully, add a few extra little personal touches, put a checkmark opposite the best two or three, and leave the list on the telephone stand, not forgetting to cross off each excuse after it was used.

The next time I met Leon he was full of thanks for my help. "As usual the Fultons called about Saturday, and I made it that one about a relative's brush with death in an auto accident which would require my immediate departure. Did you know that actually happened to my sister two years ago? It was during a rainstorm on Interstate Five. And I remembered all the details so well that no suspicion was possible." Leon had gone on to try two more of those copouts with equal success, and for the first time in months he and his family had enjoyed two whole weekends alone at home and without a ripple of ill feeling from anywhere.

(I must add as a postscript that by the time Leon and Mary finally got around to that second honeymoon, the Fultons had separated and put their house up for sale.)

Meanwhile I made up a similar list for myself and in the blink of an eye had occasion to painlessly extricate myself from a Fuller salesperson, an old friend's niece's wedding, and a Homeowner's Association wiener-bake. Though a bit frightened at my own audacity, I went on adding to my list, and as each new ploy succeeded more smoothly than the last, I soon realized that I had made a discovery perhaps no less beneficial to the comfort of my fellow creatures than the aspirin, the contraceptive pill, or that device that squelches television commercials. And there you have the germ of the four-year-long effort of research and classification and self-rummaging whose final flowering is this little book that you hold in your hands.

About the Author

ROBERT MYERS has spent most of his life in and around Los Angeles, a fertile spawning ground for excuses. After obtaining his Bachelor's degree from the University of Southern California, he was drafted and shipped to Alaska. His post-army life included stints as fry-cook, parking-lot attendant, mailman, television-script printer, insurance underwriter, advertising copywriter, and part-time poet and novelist. Receiving his Master's in English from U.C.L.A., he entered an era of stability as a technical writer for Douglas Aircraft, then eagerly shifted to college teaching, which has been his main career for the past thirteen years. Together with his wife, son, daughter, dog and cat he lives in a once-rustic but rapidly congesting Los Angeles suburb called Diamond Bar. Mr. Myers is co-author (with Anthony Garcia) of the innovative English textbook *Analogies: A Visual Approach to Writing*.